ADVANCED PLACEMENT
STUDY GUIDE

Charles Fuller
Triton College

HUMAN

GEOGRAPHY

People, Place, and Culture

Ninth Edition

H. J. de Blij
Michigan State University

Alexander B. Murphy
University of Oregon

Erin H. Fouberg
Northern State University

John Wiley & Sons, Inc.

Cover Photo: Alexander B. Murphy

To order books or for customer service, please call 1-800-CALL-WILEY (225-5945).

ISBN-13 978- 0-470-50361-4

Printed in the United States of America

10 9 8 7 6 5 4 3 2 1

Printed and bound by Bind-Rite Graphics Robbinsville, Inc.

Conquering Human Geography:
A Manual for Successful Completion of AP Human Geography
Using *Human Geography: People, Place and Culture*

Charles J. Fuller
Triton College

TABLE OF CONTENTS

PART ONE: Before You Read The Textbook

PART TWO: After You Open The Textbook

PART ONE

BEFORE YOU READ THE TEXTBOOK

A. Know Yourself and Know Your Enemy

The title of this section comes from *The Art of War*, a treatise—a systematic and extensive discourse on a subject—written by Sun-Tzu (Sunzi) in 6th century BC China. The modern and complete proverb translates to "If you know yourself and know your enemy, in a hundred battles you will have a hundred victories."

If you are reading this manual, then you are about to do battle with Advanced Placement Human Geography. The metaphor implies that you will fight many skirmishes—tests, quizzes, research projects—over the next one or two semesters, depending on how it is being taught in your school. In the end, there will be one final, epic battle—the AP Human Geography Exam. If you conquer the Exam you will get college credit for the course. Two birds with one stone, something for nothing, one course but credit in high school AND college. A good investment indeed!

The proverb above implies that success on the Exam depends on knowing yourself and knowing "the enemy," which is not really an enemy at all, just a major challenge on your path to a good education. Your family, your friends and your teachers will help you to discover the depth of your intellectual capacity and the process of realizing your potential; developing your 'inner you' is not the purpose of this student manual.

This manual will help you to "know your enemy," an enemy, by the way, that once conquered, will be your lifelong intellectual aide-de-camp. In reality, geographic literacy is an intellectual tool that will enhance all of your other talents and skills. Do not take my word for it. Many very bright people have studied the problems of geographic ignorance in the United States, and pretty much all have concluded the same thing: in this globalizing, interconnected world, remaining oblivious of other people, their cultures and their economies is not an option.

Dr. Michael P. Peterson at the Department of Geography/Geology, University of Nebraska at Omaha, summarizes nicely the importance of geography in contemporary education:

> In a world so shrunken in distance and time that you can almost instantly communicate with any other city on any other continent, and in which you can fly to virtually its remotest corner in a matter of hours, a knowledge of differing peoples and places can no longer be considered the luxury of a few, but is, instead, a necessity of every individual. Our interdependence is now so complete that business decisions taken in Tokyo or Singapore have repercussions in Copenhagen and Peoria. Just to stay abreast of world events, much less to function effectively as informed global citizens, requires that we learn not only where these events are occurring, but also why they are taking place and how they will impact on our lives. Such considerations are the very essence of geography. (Peterson)

In 2001, Secretary-General of the United Nations, Kofi Annan, addressed the Annual Meeting of the Association of American Geographers. He stated:

> Geography class is one of the first places where young people come into contact with the world beyond their immediate community. I urge you to use that platform to convey a message, not only about the carbon cycle and the wonders of our physical world, but also about political life. Please tell your students about the United Nations and its efforts to help the world address its common problems. You might also want to tell them about a new UN Web site—www.unep.net—which brings together maps, satellite images, legislation and other information from research institutions and databases

around the world. It is a powerful new way for people anywhere to monitor the environment and be involved in protecting it. (Annan)

Though I have not been able to confirm the source, I seem to recall a report on higher education that made the following important conclusion:

The World has become a more crowded, more interconnected, more volatile and more unstable place. If education cannot help students see beyond themselves and better understand the interdependent nature of our world, then each new generation will remain ignorant, and its capacity to live competently and responsibly will be dangerously diminished. . . . It is easy to understand this point in light of . . . any number of political and economic crises that have occurred in the past few decades, which emphasize the crucial nature of a globally informed citizenry. That is why we argue that . . . global education should have a high—perhaps the highest—priority.

When you get to college, you will have many opportunities to cultivate a global education: area studies courses and programs, study abroad opportunities, a chance to socialize with students from all around the world, and of course majoring in human geography. As a high school student, taking a human geography course is a great first step in the process of becoming a globally well-informed individual. You are on the right track by taking the AP Human Geography course and exam.

B.   Defining Geography

When I chose geography as my major for a doctoral degree in 1990, I assumed I knew something about the discipline, and presumed that the field was well understood by most people. Not so! I learned that to a professional or academic geographer, the discipline has meanings that transcend just knowing where things are located, although that is part of it. Fortunately at the University of Georgia, all graduate students coming into the program from a different discipline (mine was Chinese Language and East Asian Studies) were required to take a seminar that met once a week. One of its implied functions was to train us to answer the question: What is Geography? That course has come in handy many times. Often when I tell someone that I am a geographer, they respond with, "Yeah, sure, geography . . . (awkward pause) . . . what IS geography?"

Turns out very few people, even among the better educated ones, have a clear notion of what geography is. So before you tackle AP Human Geography, let's talk about geography as an academic field, but just briefly. After all, *Human Geography: People, Place and Culture* opens with a whole chapter on the question: What is Human Geography?

I will give you my personal definition in a moment, but first, let us Google the phrase "define geography." Lots of web sites appear, but one in particular—http://wordnet.princeton.edu/ perl/webwn—listed many definitions and their sources, among which were these:

- Study of the earth's surface; includes people's responses to topography and climate and soil and vegetation.
- Geography is the scientific study of the locational and spatial variation in both physical and human phenomena on Earth.
- This category includes the entries dealing with the natural environment and the effects of human activity.
- Geography is the study of the Earth's surface.

- Where are the ruins of the ancient city of Troy located? Which country was formerly known as Gold Coast?
- The science or the study of Earth and its life; a description of land, sea, air and the distribution of plant and animal life including people and cities.
- Geography has a significant impact on coffee flavor. There are three main coffee-growing regions in the world.
- Knowledge of principles and methods for describing the features of land, sea, and air masses, including their physical characteristics, locations, interrelationships, and distribution of plant, animal, and human life.
- The science of space and place that brings together Earth's physical and human dimensions in the integrated study of people, places, and environments.
- The study of physical features and natural factors like climate, soil and vegetation.
- Geography indicates the world region, country, state/province, and city.
- There is a section devoted to minerals. Kids will also enjoy the section on volcanoes and fossils. I always wondered how caves form.
- The science and art of describing, analyzing, explaining, and interpreting the Earth as the home of human beings; geography places special emphasis on the spatial relations of society and the physical or natural environment.
- A field of study based on understanding the phenomena capable of being described and analyzed with a GIS.
- The science of the Earth's surface, physical features, climate, population, etc.
- The study of the Earth's surface and its related physical, biological and cultural features.

You may have already learned the difference between qualitative and quantitative research methods, and if not, it will eventually be part of your education. Let us say for now that qualitative research methodologies try to understand what is real in the world, what people really mean by what they say or write or do. It is a more subjective approach to research than are quantitative methods (statistics-based, number-crunching methodologies), and perhaps less scientific. But good qualitative research reveals underlying structures of actual behavior that quantitative methods often miss in their search for generalizations.

One particular type of qualitative research is called "content analysis." The content analysis approach to research is based on analyzing human communications, whether oral or written. I found one pithy definition online:

> Any technique for making inferences by objectively and systematically identifying specified characteristics of messages. (http://pareonline.net/getvn.asp?v=7&n=17)

I used a similar methodology in my doctoral dissertation as a way to determine possible explanations for China's export patterns.

What "message" are the authors of the above definitions of geography trying to convey? A superfluous analysis reveals several recurrent themes. Distilling them out (in content analysis it is often called 'coding'), we find the following characteristics:

Geography:
- is the scientific study of the Earth's surface
- studies the interactions between people and their physical environments
- focuses on the locational and spatial variations of phenomena, both human and non-human (so-called natural or physical/biological)

- is descriptive, i.e., describes a phenomenon, where it is located, and how it is related to other phenomena
- identifies regions (again, both human/cultural and physical/biological regions)
- describes, analyzes, explains and interprets

There is one key word not mentioned in these descriptions of the field, a term that is an essential part of any definition of geography: **pattern**. Pattern refers to spatial patterns, which is another way of saying geographic patterns. Like all definitions of complex things, there are plenty of variations, but here is a basic definition: The geometric or regular arrangement of something in a study area (Rubenstein). I also seem to recall another terse definition: a detectable organization of spatial units (if you find the source, let me know). Similar terms in geography include spatial structure and spatial organization. But I get ahead of myself.

In my course syllabi I have been using this definition of geography:

> Geography is the systematic study of the spatial patterns of all phenomena on or near the Earth's surface. Its primary methodology is spatial analysis which asks two basic questions: **where** are things located (spatial), and **why** are they located where they are (analysis). Its primary tool of communication is the map.

That is my "original" introductory definition of geography, however, it is obviously informed by all other attempts. Of course any definition can be refined ad infinitum, but for now I think these simple definitions will suffice. If you get a college and/or graduate degree in geography some day, no doubt you will want to render your own succinct definition. By the time you finish this introduction and read the first chapter of *Human Geography: People, Place, and Culture* you will be more qualified than most people to answer the question: What is Geography?

C. National Geography Standards

What happens when many eminent geographers in education, government and the private sector, in cooperation with the premier geography related organizations of America, get together to hash out what they consider to be the quintessence—the essence of a thing in its purest form—of geographic education? A book, of course, but one that serves as something of a Holy Writ for geography teachers. The book, *Geography for Life: National Geography Standards 1994*, has for more than a decade served as the guidepost for those who design geography curricula. Your teacher should have a copy. Ask her (or him) if you can borrow it. Better yet, ask her if your school can get copies for all of your classmates, or at least put a couple of copies in the school library.

As for the eminent geographers and institutions responsible for the publication, I defer to Roger M. Downs:

> The National Geography Standards were produced under the sponsorship of the four major geography organizations: the American Geographical Society, the Association of American Geographers, the National Council for Geographic Education, and the National Geographic Society. Thus they are a statement not only for all the people interested in geography but also for all the major players in geography education.

> The standards are a consensus statement, produced in a way that allowed as many people as possible as many opportunities as possible to shape the document. Over a two-year writing period, 140 people worked on the six drafts that led to *Geography for Life*. These people included K-12 teachers from public and private schools, school

4

administrators and PTA members, college and university faculty, and government and business officials. Another 216 people responded in writing to these drafts, and 130 people testified at nine public hearings.

source: http://www.nationalgeographic.com/education/standards.html

The collective wisdom of all these people resulted in eighteen geography standards. The following table is the summary of these standards from *Geography for Life*. Don't panic!! No one expects you to immediately know exactly what the standards mean. That is one of the reasons you are taking this course, besides the possibility of college credit. After the course, after you have digested the information in the textbook, *Human Geography: People, Place, and Culture*, I am confident that you will have a strong understanding and appreciation of the standards.

The Eighteen Geography Standards

ESSENTIAL ELEMENT	STANDARDS
THE WORLD IN SPATIAL TERMS Geography studies relationships between people, places, and environments by mapping information about them into a spatial context.	1. How to use maps and other geographic representations, tools and technologies to acquire, process and report information from a spatial perspective. 2. How to use mental maps to organize information about people, places, and environments in a spatial context. 3. How to analyze the spatial organization of people, places, and environments on Earth's surface.
PLACES AND REGIONS The identities and lives of individuals and peoples are rooted in particular places in those human constructs called regions.	4. The physical and human characteristics of places. 5. That people create regions to interpret earth's complexity. 6. How culture and experience influence people's perceptions of places and regions
PHYSICAL SYSTEMS Phys. processes shape Earth's surface and interact with plant and animal life to create, sustain, and modify ecosystems.	7. The physical processes that shape the patterns of Earth's surface. 8. The characteristics and spatial distribution of ecosystems on Earth's surface.
HUMAN SYSTEMS People are central to geography in that human activities help shape Earth's surface, human settlements and structures are part of Earth's surface, and humans compete for control of Earth's surface.	9. The characteristics, distribution, and migration of human population on Earth's surface. 10. The characteristics, distribution, and complexity of Earth's cultural mosaics.

	11. The patterns and networks of economic interdependence on Earth's surface. 12. The processes, patterns, and functions of human settlement. 13. How the forces of cooperation and conflict among people influence human control of Earth's surface.
ENVIRONMENT AND SOCIETY The physical environment is modified by human activities, largely as a consequence of the ways in which human societies value and use Earth's natural resources, and human activities are also influenced by Earth's physical features and processes.	14. How human actions modify the physical environment. 15. How physical systems affect human systems. 16. The changes that occur in meaning, use, distribution and importance of resources.
THE USES OF GEOGRAPHY Knowledge of geography enables people to develop an understanding of the relationships between people, places, and environments over time--that is, of Earth as it was, is, and might be.	17. How to apply geography to interpret the past. 18. How to apply geography to interpret the present and plan for the future.

source: The Geography Education Standards Project. 1994. *Geography for Life: National Geography Standards, 1994.* Washington, DC. National Geographic Research & Exploration.

D. The AP Human Geography Course and Exam

1. Course Description

Back to the metaphor of knowing yourself and knowing your enemy. There is a small booklet called *AP Human Geography: Course Description* published by the College Board. It contains a lot of information on the APHG course and test. You can download it for free at:

http://www.collegeboard.com/student/testing/ap/sub_humangeo.html?humangeo

Your teacher probably has a printed copy, but you can save a digital copy to you computer, or read it online, or print out a copy for yourself if you prefer reading the old-fashioned way—holding the printed text right there in your hands. Having an idea about how the course and test is structured, the topics covered on the exam, and samples of both multiple choice and free response questions—that is tantamount to knowing your 'enemy.' In other words, you will have an advantage on the Big Exam if you are familiar with the standards used in the design of the test. If you read this publication early in the course, then as you read *Human Geography: People, Place, and Culture* you will have a better idea of what to look for and on what to focus.

The people who designed the APHG Exam based the content on five college-level goals that build on the above National Geography Standards. As the booklet points out, if you successfully complete the course and do well on The Exam, you should be able to do the following:

- **Use and Think About Maps and Spatial Data**. Geography is fundamentally concerned with the ways in which patterns on Earth's surface reflect and influence physical and human processes. As such, maps and spatial data are fundamental to the discipline, and learning to use and think about them is critical to geographical literacy. The goal is achieved when students learn to use maps and spatial data to pose and solve problems, and when they learn to think critically about what is revealed and what is hidden in different maps and spatial arrays.

- **Understand and Interpret Implications of Associations Among Phenomena in Places**. Geography looks at the world from a spatial perspective—seeking to understand the changing spatial organization and material character of Earth's surface. One of the critical advantages of a spatial perspective is the attention it focuses on how phenomena are related to one another in particular places. Students should thus learn not just to recognize and interpret patterns, but also to assess the nature and significance of the relationships among phenomena that occur in the same place, and to understand how tastes and values, political regulations, and economic constraints work together to create particular types of cultural landscapes.

- **Recognize and Interpret at Different Scales Relationships Among Patterns and Processes**. Geographical analysis requires a sensitivity to scale—not just as a spatial category but as a framework for understanding how events and processes at different scales influence one another. Thus, students should understand that the phenomena they are studying at one scale (e.g., local) may well be influenced by developments at other scales (e.g., regional, national, or global). They should then look at processes operating at multiple scales when seeking explanations of geographic patterns and arrangements.

- **Define Regions and Evaluate the Regionalization Process**. Geography is concerned not simply with describing patterns, but with analyzing how they came about and what they mean. Students should see regions as objects of analysis and exploration and move beyond simply locating and describing regions to considering how and why they come into being—and what they reveal about the changing character of the world in which we live.

- **Characterize and Analyze Changing Interconnections Among Places**. At the heart of a geographical perspective is a concern with the ways in which events and processes operating in one place can influence those operating at other places. Thus, students should view places and patterns not in isolation, but in terms of their spatial and functional relationship with other places and patterns. Moreover, they should strive to be aware that those relationships are constantly changing, and they should understand how and why change occurs.

I can assure you that if you do achieve the level of geographic competence implied in the above goals, even if you never take another geography course, you will have intellectual tools that will enhance all of the other skills you accumulate over time.

2. The Topics and Topic Outline

The *AP Human Geography: Course Description* provides a short statement on seven key topics that they expect qualified APHG teachers to cover in the course. There is no need to repeat them here since you can do that easily enough by accessing the whole booklet online. I will, however, provide for you the Topic Outline. This not only shows you the major topics covered on the Exam, it also estimates the proportion of multiple choice questions (MCQs) in each content area.

Let me reiterate an important point. As you look over this course outline, you are apt to be a little intimidated. So many unfamiliar ideas! So many new terms! Rest assured that you are already employing many of these ideas in your daily activities, you are just not aware of it. Have you ever had an inchoative feeling or idea that frustrated you because you did not have the vocabulary to express it? Inchoative, by the way, means not yet clearly or completely formed or organized. Much of what we do or think in life has spatial characteristics. Geography, the academic discipline, provides the language that will enable you to crystallize those ideas that are spatial in nature. The more you read the news—domestic and international—and follow current events, the more you will realize how much of this outline you already intuitively understand.

One more point. As you read your textbook, *Human Geography: People, Place, and Culture*, return frequently to this outline. It will help you to focus on that part of the textbook content that has a good chance of finding its way into the APHG Exam.

AP Human Geography Topic Outline	
Content Area (Subject)	**Percentage Goals for Exam**

I.   Geography: Its Nature and Perspectives
A.   Geography as a field of inquiry
B.   Evolution of key geographical concepts and models associated with notable geographers
C.   Key concepts underlying the geographical perspective: location, space, place, scale, pattern, regionalization, and globalization
D.   Key geographical skills
   1.   How to use and think about maps and spatial data
   2.   How to understand and interpret the implications of associations among phenomena in places
   3.   How to recognize and interpret at different scales the relationships among patterns and processes
   4.   How to define regions and evaluate the regionalization process
   5.   How to characterize and analyze changing interconnections among places
E.   New geographic technologies, such as GIS and GPS
F.   Sources of geographical ideas and data: the field, census data
	5-10%

II.   Population
A.   Geographical analysis of population
   1.   Density, distribution and scale
   2.   Consequences of various densities and distributions
   3.   Patterns of compositions: age, sex, race, and ethnicity
   4.   Population and natural hazards: past, present, and future
	13-17%

B. Population growth and decline over time and space
1. Historical trends and projections for the future
2. Theories of population growth, including the Demographic Model
3. Patterns of fertility, mortality, and health
4. Regional variations of demographic transitions
5. Effects of population choices
C. Population movement
1. Push and pull factors
2. Major voluntary and involuntary migrations at different scales
3. Migration selectivity
4. Short-term, local movements, and activity space

III. Cultural Patterns and Processes   13-17%
A. Concepts of culture
1. Traits
2. Diffusion
3. Acculturation
4. Cultural regions
B. Cultural differences
1. Language
2. Religion
3. Ethnicity
4. Gender
5. Popular and folk culture
C. Environmental impacts of cultural attitudes and practices
D. Cultural landscapes and cultural identity
1. Values and preferences
2. Symbolic landscapes and sense of place

IV. Political Organization of Space   13-17%
A. Territorial dimensions of politics
1. The concept of territoriality
2. The nature and meaning of boundaries
3. Influences of boundaries on identity, interaction, and exchange
B. Evolution of the contemporary political pattern
1. The nation-state concept
2. Colonialism and imperialism
3. Federal and unitary states
C. Challenges to inherited political-territorial arrangements
1. Changing nature of sovereignty
2. Fragmentation, unification, alliance
3. Spatial relationships between political patterns and patterns of ethnicity, economy, and environment
4. Electoral geography, including gerrymandering

V. Agricultural and Rural Land Use   13-17%
A. Development and diffusion of agriculture
1. Neolithic Agricultural Revolution
2. Second Agricultural Revolution
B. Major agricultural production regions
1. Agricultural systems associated with major bioclimatic zones

       2.   Variations within major zones and effects of markets
       3.   Linkages and flows among regions of food production and
           consumption
   C. Rural land use and settlement patterns
       1.   Models of agricultural land use, including von Thünen's Model
       2.   Settlement patterns associated with major agricultural types
   D. Modern commercial agriculture
       1.   Third Agricultural Revolution
       2.   Green Revolution
       3.   Biotechnology
       4.   Spatial organization and diffusion of industrial agriculture
       5.   Future food supplies and environmental impacts of agriculture

VI. Industrialization and Economic Development   13-17%
   A. Key concepts in industrialization and development
   B. Growth and diffusion of industrialization
       1.   The changing roles of energy and technology
       2.   Industrial Revolution
       3.   Evolution of economic cores and peripheries
       4.   Geographic critiques of models of economic localization (i.e.,
           land rent, comparative costs of transportation), industrial
           location, economic development, and world systems
   C. Contemporary patterns and impacts of industrialization and
      development
       1.   Spatial organization of the world economy
       2.   Variations in levels of development
       3.   Deindustrialization and economic restructuring
       4.   Pollution, health, and quality of life
       5.   Industrialization, environmental change, and sustainability
       6.   Local development initiatives: government policies

VII. Cities and Urban Land Use   13-17%
   A. Definitions of urbanism
   B. Origin and evolution of cities
       1.   Historical patterns of urbanization
       2.   Rural-urban migration and urban growth
       3.   Global cities and megacities
       4.   Models of urban systems
   C. Functional character of contemporary cities
       1.   Changing employment mix
       2.   Changing demographic and social structures
   D. Built environment and social space
       1.   Comparative models of internal city structure
       2.   Transportation and infrastructure
       3.   Political organization of urban areas
       4.   Urban planning and design
       5.   Patterns of race, ethnicity, gender, and class
       6.   Uneven development, ghettoization, and gentrification
       7.   Impacts of suburbanization and edge cities

source: College Board. 2005. *AP Human Geography Course Description.*

3. Developing the APHG Test

I am somewhat reluctant to drop another publication on you, but if you really want to "know your enemy," there is an article about the APHG course and exam written by Adrian J. Bailey that I think you should read, or have your teacher read it and explain it to you (it is a bit on the technical side). The article, "What Kind of Assessment for What Kind of Geography? Advanced Placement Human Geography" (Bailey 2006) appeared in the February 2006 edition of *The Professional Geographer*, one of the two academic geography journals published by the Association of American Geographers (AAG). If your teacher does not receive the *Journal* but you would like a copy of the article, you might contact the publisher directly:

> *The Professional Geographer*
> Association of American Geographers
> 1710 16th Street NW
> Washington, DC 20009
> Voice: (202) 234-1450 Fax: (202) 234-2744
> E-mail: profgeog@aag.org
> http://www.aag.org/Publications/pgweb1.html

In the article, Dr. Bailey describes the process whereby the APHG Exam was conceived, developed and implemented. He writes about the challenges faced by the Test Development Committee (TDC) whose task it was to develop a syllabus and method of assessment for the new course. In the development of the Exam, the TDC was guided by five considerations:

> 1. Design a regime (a regulated system) that gave students opportunities to demonstrate both the breadth of their knowledge and their ability and confidence in applying a skills portfolio.
>
> 2. The regime should not statistically disadvantage students by dint of their sex, ethnic origin, or exposure to specific elements of the course outline.
>
> 3. Consistent with the AP ethos, assessment needed to generate reliable data that enabled clear performance bands to be identified.
>
> 4. To establish legitimacy, APHG standards needed to track college geography standards over time.
>
> 5. The exam had to be of a length that was consistent with the goal of giving the course equivalence with a one-semester college offering. (72)

I am sharing these course and test development criteria with you as a lead-in to the section of Dr. Bailey's article titled "Question Design." After all, in addition to mastering the information in the textbook, that is, the process whereby information in the textbook becomes knowledge you will retain, it will not hurt to have some idea about how questions are conceived and designed.

I should also point out that there are two kinds of questions on the Exam presented in two sections:

> Section 1: Multiple Choice Questions (MCQs)
> Section 2: Free Response Questions (FRQs).

The APHG Exam consists of 75 multiple choice questions that must be completed in 60 minutes, and three multiple-part free response questions that also must be completed in 60 minutes (you should budget about twenty minutes per FRQ).

The MCQs used in the APHG Exam are contributed by a large number of college professors and instructors who teach introductory human geography courses. I submitted a few myself some years ago, but have no idea if any of them were actually selected; they, the College Board and APHG Test Development Committee, must have thousands of multiple choice questions from which to choose. Before a question makes it into the Exam, it is field tested in college classrooms.

Dr. Bailey, who by the way was the Chief Reader of the APHG Exam for its first five years—a swell guy with an English accent and great sense of humor (humour in England)—writes that the selection of MCQs is guided by three considerations:

1.   Of the seventy-five questions on any Exam, fifteen are carried forward to the next administration of the Exam. This way the TDC can get an impression of the ability levels of different groups of students sitting for different versions of the test.

2.   To assess breadth of knowledge, the overall structure of the MCQ section reflects the content structure of the course. (Which is a good reason you should look over Table 2 above).

3.   The test must have an acceptable distribution of questions ranked by difficulty, which is determined by field testing of the questions.

No doubt you have already been exposed to hundreds, probably thousands of multiple choice questions in your decade or more of school. While thousands of teachers write millions of questions every year, in fact, good MCQs are not easy to compose. There is a nice, short essay on the virtues of MCQs by Dr. Russell A. Dewey at Georgia Southern University. You can view this essay at:

http://www.psywww.com/selfquiz/aboutq.htm.

Unlike the average teacher who probably generates MCQs without thorough consideration of their format, you can rest assured that no MCQ will make it to the APHG exam until it has been exhaustively scrutinized and tested. MCQ formats may well include: basic knowledge; application; and analysis, synthesis and evaluation. These formats with samples are nicely summarized at:

http://www.pepraxis.com/0091/understandmc.htm

Regarding the Free Response Questions section of the Exam, Dr. Bailey writes:

In general terms, one FR item gives students an opportunity to elaborate on cause and effect relationships. A second FR item on a given test calls upon skills of synthesis and rewards students who can draw on materials from different course sections to respond to the question. A third FR item may test ability to apply geographic skills or critically appraise abstract concepts, or both (Bailey, 72-73).

In summary, so much thought and planning and testing has gone into the APHG Exam design that when you get your 3 or 4 or 5 score on the Exam (roughly equivalent to a college C or B or A), you know you have done some righteous work for which you can be truly proud. My honest assessment, based on APHG teachers I have met and their syllabi I have read, is that the APHG course is often taught more robustly—more rich and full—than it is in college.

4. Sample Questions from the Released Exam

I just happen to have a copy of the released 2001 AP Human Geography Released Exam. Inside the front cover is a statement that says:

> These materials are intended for noncommercial use by AP teachers for course and exam preparation. Teachers may reproduce them, in whole or in part, for limited use with their students, but may not mass-produce the materials, electronically or otherwise.

I cannot imagine a better way to mentally and intellectually prepare for the APHG Exam than by doing a test run using the 2001 Exam (or subsequently released versions). Your teacher is allowed to make copies for classroom use. I suggest you "take" the released exam a couple of weeks before you take the real Exam. There are two clear benefits by doing a trial test: 1) You will become familiar and comfortable with the types of questions you will see on the Exam, and 2) this way you will not have to waste valuable seconds or minutes after opening the test booklet trying to understand the instructions and test format. Yes, when you take the actual Exam read the instructions carefully! However, since you will have "taken" the test once, you will be able to assimilate the instructions more quickly.

Unfortunately, the College Board refused permission to use a few of their questions from the 2001 Exam in this manual. Ask you teacher to obtain a copy, which can be ordered from:

http://store.collegeboard.com/productdetail.do?Itemkey=994585

As mentioned in their cover statement, your teacher will then be able to make copies for classroom use. The following observations will make more sense when you have the questions in front of you.

Often a question—or series of questions—will be accompanied by a picture or graph or diagram. For example, on the 2001 Exam, number 6 was accompanied by a pen drawing of a "saltbox-type house," and number 8 was accompanied by an outline map of Western Europe and North Africa with flow lines of various thicknesses drawn from peripheral regions to France and Germany. Therefore it is a good idea to study all of the figures in *Human Geography: People, Place and Culture*—maps, graphs, tables, models—and know how to apply them to situations different from the example given in the textbook.

I was under the impression that the College Board generally eschews (shuns; avoids) *negative response* questions, those with EXCEPT, NOT or LEAST in the question. On the 2001 Exam, however, I found five. Negative response questions can be tricky to interpret; often the "right" answer is determined by a process of elimination, i.e., if four of the five responses in fact support the statement, the fifth one will be the "right" answer by virtue of it being a wrong association.

Some of the questions are straight forward *basic knowledge* type questions; either you know the answer or you do not—though you might be able to successfully conjecture—make an educated guess—a correct answer. *Application* type questions expect you to use basic knowledge in context, thus going beyond simple memorization of facts.

The most difficult type of MCQ is the *analysis, synthesis and evaluation* type question. These are questions based on hypothetical situations in which your knowledge of geographical principles can be used to correctly surmise (same as conjecture) the answer. I did not see any of this type of question in the MCQ section of the 2001 Released Exam. Not to worry, wait till you see the three Free Response questions!

Not being able to share with you here any of the free response questions from the 2001 Released Exam, all I can tell you is that they are usually written in multiple parts and require you to synthesize information that will be learned over several chapters and topics. When I first typed out the questions, and my initial reaction was "Whew! Just typing those FR questions challenges my brain."

Let us analyze the third free response question, which your teacher should make available to you. First is the assumption that you studied the Rostow model of development, as well as its strengths and weaknesses vis-à-vis its ability to predict the development trajectories of Less Developed Countries. The question gives you the essence of the model—the Five Stages, but it does not tell you whether or not it is a good model, i.e., whether or not all Less Developed Countries will follow—or can expect to follow—the same path of development as the More Developed Countries did. So if you have NOT studied the Rostow model, all is not lost, but you will be handicapped.

Next notice that you have to interpret the Rostow model's viability relative to four areas of inquiry, (a) through (d), of which you get to select three. You will not find these answers in any single chapter of *Human Geography: People, Place and Culture*. Rostow's model is covered in Chapter 10, but you will need to have assimilated—to absorb into one's thinking—knowledge from several other chapters, such as:

14: Globalization and the Geography of Networks (world economy);
 8: Political Geography (colonialism);
 4: Local Culture, Popular Culture, and Cultural Landscapes (cultural differences); and
 5: Identity: Race, Ethnicity, Gender and Sexuality (social and class structures).

If that were not enough, you then have to synthesize—to bring together into a whole—the whole thing relative to three world regions: Latin America, Sub-Saharan Africa, and South Asia. Is that a challenge or what!

Fortunately it can be done. The 2001 Released Exam in fact gives a sample of a student answer to each of the FR questions. It gives you an overview of the question and the key points for which the AP readers (the people scoring the answers) are looking based on a rubric—a set of scoring criteria—that all readers use. There is also a commentary, probably by the Chief Reader, that explains what he or she liked or did not like about the answer—kind of like the judges on American Idol.

IMPORTANT! While it is always good to write in polished prose, you will be pressed for time, and the quality of your writing has no bearing on the final score. Read the FR question, analyze it for a minute or so, do not rush into writing. Jot down a couple of key ideas, juggle the pieces in your mind till they fit coherently and cohesively. Then use sparse but clear diction to answer the question; lay off unnecessary adjectives.

5. Feedback from APHG Teachers

As a college instructor, I teach a standard human geography course. But I have never taught an APHG course. I want you to have the best advice on how to succeed, so I asked many experienced APHG teachers one question: What is the one best technique you use that helps students get the most from the APHG class, especially in the use of the textbook *Human Geography: People, Place, and Culture*? Fourteen teachers responded.

Once again applying a little qualitative analysis to their responses, here is what I discovered. I selected key words or phrases from the lengthy text messages these teachers sent me. I "coded" these words and phrases by choosing a single word that I felt characterized a cluster of similar terms.

The fun part about qualitative analysis is deciding what all of this means. Coding these teacher responses was a very simple project, and I think mostly self-explanatory. Our first conclusion (see the following table) is that eight of the fourteen teachers felt making the concepts in the textbook "real" was an effective way to succeed in the course. How do they do that? Usually by taking a geographic principle as explained in the textbook and applying it to the real world, that is, finding within current events examples of phenomena that can be better understood through a geographic perspective. Some teachers have students do case studies, some use newspapers and/or CNN as ancillary learning materials. If you want to get the most from the textbook, then you should not just read the book, you should also be an avid follower of current events, both domestic and international. I personally suggest you use your MP3/FM Tuner device to listen to National Public Radio (NPR) on your way to school and on the way home.

Code	Frequency	Related Terms
Relevance	8	case study, contemporary issues, real data, relevancy, real world events, current events, links events to textbook, world affairs
Discussion	5	class discussion, talk, Socratic dialog, Socratic discussion, discussion
Visuals	5	graphics, images, videos, visual approach, visual
Models	3	models, models, theories
Reading	2	read chapters, get students to read
Vocabulary	2	key terms, vocabulary
Outline	2	outline, outline chapters
Others	1 X 4	Cornell Note method, study guides, scale, frequent quizzes

Teachers also mentioned engaging in regular discussions in class. One of the differences between high school and college is that in college, especially in freshmen and sophomore classes, professors will often lecture to 200-300 students. There may be little opportunity to engage in discussions or debates in class. One of the most successful APHG teachers I know (that is, most of her students score high on the APHG Exam) told me that the students are expected to read the textbook on their own, and she quizzes them every week. But she never lectures from the book, her classes are forums for the exchange of ideas.

It seems many people are, or claim to be, "visual learners." These are people who learn best by using visual stimulation. Fortunately for them geography is a very visual discipline. In fact, a geographer's main tool of communication is the map, which by its nature is a visual communication device ("If a picture paints a thousand words . . ."). We also use lots of charts and graphs and tables and models. Take a few seconds and flip though *Human Geography: People, Place, and Culture*; it seems as if the page space devoted to graphics is nearly as much as the space devoted to text. In fact, I sometimes use the textbook DVD from John Wiley & Sons (the textbook publisher), which contains all of the photos and figures in the textbook, as my lecture notes. It is not surprising, then, that several of the teachers said that visuals (graphics, images, videos) were an essential part of APHG success. In the preface of the textbook you will find that John Wiley & Sons provides you with numerous audio and visual resources to enhance the learning experience.

Even though only a few teachers mentioned reading, vocabulary, outlining chapters, and using study guides as important elements of success, this does not diminish their importance. I posit (assume as fact) that the MOST important activity is reading—not looking at pictures. Even in this age of staccato visual stimulation (music videos being a prime example), you must be a reader and the master of language to expect any kind of success in life. Visual aids can reinforce learning, but real learning comes by assimilating knowledge through reading.

E.   Analyzing the Textbook

Based on my own experience both as a student and a teacher, I have three recommendations to help you get the most from *Human Geography: People, Place, and Culture*.

- Read all of the front material.
- Outline each chapter before you read it.
- As you read the textbook, mark all over it. Wait! Before you actually deface the book based on my recommendation, read what I have to say about that below.

1.   Front Material

One of the first things you should do when you get your copy of *People, Place and Culture* is to read all of the front material, which is essentially the Preface and a section About the Authors.

The **Preface** tells you a little about the book, about how it is organized, about what changes have been made since the last edition, and so on. It also has a subsection called Resources That Help Students Learn. There is a link to a Student Companion Website which you should visit: www.wiley.com/college/deblij. Reading the Preface is kind of like meeting someone for the first time; your first impressions of the book will come from the Preface. Maybe a better analogy is the opening lines of a novel. A good preface, like a good opening line ("It was a dark and stormy night . . . ") will draw you into the book.

Get to know the **Authors**. If you read their short biographies, you will discover (I hope) that the authors are cool people. I have not actually met them myself, but I know of them; they are highly respected geographers. They all have great reputations as teachers and scholars. They have all traveled extensively around the world. They all can talk the arcane (impenetrable) language of people with a very advanced education, but they have not forgotten how to communicate with young people. If you would meet them, you would probably like them. As you read the textbook, especially their Field Notes, imagine them "in the field," on site in some exotic location. That could be you someday.

2. Outline the Chapters

Before you start reading a chapter, flip through it, then write up *by hand* a complete outline of the hierarchical subject headings. I suggest by hand because you are more likely to be thinking about what you are writing, and you will be dwelling on section titles a bit longer than if you are typing them on a computer (especially if you are a good touch-typist and do not actually have to ruminate on the letters and words you are typing). Outlining a chapter and contemplating the section headings gives you the broad idea of what is to be covered in the chapter. You will not necessarily understand the implications of the titles, but you will be planting intellectual seeds that will sprout after watering them with focused reading. (Don't you just love a good metaphor?)

It does not really matter what method of outlining you use, but it is important to be systematic and consistent. Most textbooks, and I dare say all well-written ones, have no more than three levels of hierarchy in a chapter:

- first level, a major subject title
  - second level, a sub-section title subsumed under the main subject
    - third level, a sub-sub-section title subsumed under the second level

Any more levels of organization and it is easy to lose track of the original organizing theme. I have provided below a couple of outline styles for your consideration. There are others, or you may create your own. Just keep it simple and consistent.

Chapter 1: Introduction to Human Geography

A. What Is Human Geography?
B. What Are Geographic Questions?
    1. Maps in the Time of Cholera Pandemics
    2. The Spatial Perspective
       a. The Five Themes
       b. Cultural Landscape
C. Why Do Geographers Use Maps, and What Do Maps Tell Us?
    1. Mental Maps
    2. Generalization in Maps
    3. Remote Sensing and GIS
D. Why Are Geographers Concerned with Scale and Connectedness?
    1. Regions
       Perceptual Regions in the United States
    2. Culture
    3. Connectedness Through Diffusion
       a. Expansion Diffusion
       b. Relocation Diffusion
E. What Are Geographic Concepts, and How Are They Used in Answering Geographic Questions?
    1. Environmental Determinism
    2. Positivism
    3. Today's Human Geography

Chapter 2: Population

1. Where In The World Do People Live?
   1.1. Physiologic Population Density
   1.2. Population Distribution
   1.3. World Population Distribution and Density
        1.3.1. East Asia
        1.3.2. South Asia
        1.3.3. Europe
        1.3.4. North America
   1.4. Reliability of Population Data
2. Why Do Populations Rise and Fall in Particular Places?
   2.1. Population Growth at World, Regional, National, and Local Scales
        2.1.1. Population Growth at the Regional and National Scales
        2.1.2. Population Growth at the Local Scale
   2.2. The Demographic Transition in Great Britain
   2.3. The Demographic Transition
        2.3.1. Stage 1: Low Growth
        2.3.2. Stage 2: High Growth
        2.3.3. Stage 3: Moderate Growth
        2.3.4. Stage 4: Low Growth or Stationary Stage (wrong print color/font)
   2.4. Future Population Growth
3. Why Does Population Composition Matter?
   3.1. Infant Mortality
   3.2. Child Mortality
   3.3. Life Expectancy
   3.4. AIDS
   3.5. The Maladies of Longer Life Expectancy
4. How Do Governments Affect Population Change?
   4.1. Limitations
   4.2. Contradictions

One of the basic principles of outlining is that at any level in the outline hierarchy, there should be at least two section topics. Therefore if you have a section A, there must also be a section B. Within A, if you have a subsection 1. then you must have a subsection 2. Within a subsection 1. if you have a subsection a. then you must also have a subsection b. A well-structured textbook makes it a lot easier to connect the information in a chapter. Generally speaking, *Human Geography: People, Place, and Culture* does an excellent job of organizing its material hierarchically, but do not be too picky if the textbook itself does not follow the rules of outlining perfectly (I have found several cases where they have, for example, a level *a* but no *b*).

3. Mark Up the Book

When you get to college and you are on a tight budget, spending $100 or more for a textbook can hurt financially. (Hint: start saving now). So most students, hoping to return their textbooks at the end of the semester for a maximum refund—usually only about 15% of the original purchase price—do not put any marks in or on their books; they do not underline important passages, they do not highlight probable testable ideas, they do not fold over the corners of pages with critical tables, they do not scribble in the margins reminders to call someone for a date. If that's you, there is a good chance you are not assimilating very much knowledge from the textbook. I personally feel that any book worth reading is worth marking up, textbooks, novels, encyclopedias, etc.

BUT . . . that would be OK only if you actually own the book. The books you use in high school and in libraries are not yours, they belong to the school district or the school itself, and the district plans to use them for several years. Marking them up would be frowned upon, so you do not have the right to mark them up. You need to come up with an alternative. One alternative is time-consuming, but actually helps you to retain the information. Take notes as you read.

F. Critical Thinking

I have read somewhere that information does not become knowledge until we think critically about it. If so, a textbook does not give you knowledge, rather it is nothing more than a mass of systematically arranged information. Memorizing thousands of bits of information may help you do reasonably well on the APHG Exam multiple choice questions, but it will not help you much on the free response questions. For those you will have to think critically. We hear that a lot, but what IS critical thinking? Check out: http://www.criticalreading.com/critical_thinking.htm

If by Exam time you have indeed become a geographically well-informed person, then you will have acquired a set of powerful geographic skills that will enable you to think critically about phenomena with spatial ramifications (consequences, outgrowth). In *Geography for Life*, we anticipate acquiring the following skills. You will be able to:
- ask geographic questions
- acquire geographic information
- organize geographic information
- analyze geographic information
- answer geographic questions

These are the skills of a person capable of critical thinking, skills that will be critical in answering the Free Response Questions on the APHG Exam. As you saw above, the FRQ usually have multiple parts that require you to contemplate the nature of separate ideas, and then elucidate on how they are holistically interconnected.

G. Final Remark

For most working people, and that includes students, our scarcest resource is time. I know I have suggested a lot of work that is going to cut into your social time, and even take away from some of your other non-AP courses. Nonetheless, if you do not make a major effort to conquer AP Human Geography and the Exam, you will probably still get high school credit, but you may not do well enough on the Exam to get college credit. Is that not, after all, the goal, to get two things for the price of one? To take this one course now and get both high school AND college credit? Take enough AP classes successfully in high school, and you can save a whole semester of college—college tuition, textbook costs, maybe graduate in three-and-a-half years instead of four (or, nowadays, more likely five). Taking AP courses and taking them serious is an excellent good investment with a great return.

H. Oh! About Wikipedia

Yeah, I know. Your teachers have told you that Wikipedia is disallowed in your academic research. Wikipedia has been so maligned and negatively labeled that if it had self-awareness it would need years of counseling to gain any self-esteem. Okay, I will be the first to admit that Wikipedia is NOT a legitimate resource for doing serious research. It would be embarrassing to see Wikipedia in the bibliography or works cited section at the end of a term paper.

BUT . . . Darnit! I use Wikipedia almost daily, including in class. Not as an exclusive source of information, but for quick insights, for immediate albeit limited knowledge. Wikipedia is the product of a community of people, everyone from qualified intellectuals to self-serving charlatans—but mostly the former. If someone edits or uploads spurious (sham, bogus) or specious (erroneous, counterfactual) information, others in the community spot it and challenge it almost immediately. Wikipedia usually tells you up front if an article is challenged by the larger community.

Wikipedia is, in my opinion, a good place to start investigating a subject, just not a good place to end. Take, for example, the article on the Indus Valley Civilization (IVC):

(http://en.wikipedia.org/wiki/Indus_Valley_Civilization

I thought the article was pretty good, but if I need additional information or more serious scholarship, I look at the end of the web page. For the IVC article, there are sixty notes with sources, an extensive bibliography, and additional external links.

As you read through *Human Geography: People, Place and Culture*, you may find it very helpful to get quick additional knowledge and reinforcement from Wikipedia for some of the terms and places in the textbook. Of course there are innumerable other resources as well, online and in print, to which your teacher will direct you. But if you feel the impulse to reference Wikipedia, and your only option is a furtive (covert, hush-hush) glance under the blanket with a flashlight after everyone else has gone to sleep, you have my permission.

PART TWO:

AFTER YOU OPEN THE TEXTBOOK

INTRODUCTION

A portion of the energy used in mastering a college course is logistics—the managing of the details of an undertaking. Before beginning the detailed reading and analysis of the separate chapters of the book, take a look at the big picture—the structure of the whole book. Then before you begin to read each chapter, review the structure of that particular chapter. In this manual I have done much of the work for you.

Table of Contents for *Human Geography: People, Place, and Culture*

Your APHG teacher will give you a course syllabus. She (or he) will probably tell you how much material from the textbook you are responsible for on a week-to-week basis. Some teachers use the textbook as the primary learning resource, while others use it as a supplement. Either way, you will have to pace yourself, that is, determine how many pages from the textbook you will need to read each week.

The following table does two things for you: 1) it shows you how many pages are in each chapter, which should help with your personal logistics; 2) it is the broadest outline of the textbook, its infrastructure, and gives you an overview of the main theme of each chapter.

Note: The Appendices for the 9th edition of the textbook were not available when this workbook was being revised.

Structure of the Workbook

Each of the following chapters in this workbook corresponds to one of the chapters in the textbook. The outline for the workbook chapters is consistent:

Chapter Summary
Key Questions
Field Notes
Thinking Geographically
Chapter Outline
Chapter Figure and Tables
    Exercise for Chapter Figures and Tables
Geographic Concepts
    Quiz for Geographic Concepts
Internet Resources
    Learn More Online
    Watch It Online
APHG-Type Questions
    Multiple Choice Questions
        Type A: Basic Knowledge Questions
        Type B: Application Questions
        Free Response Questions

Chapter Summary

The Chapter Summary is a cut-and-paste job, and may be a little like putting the cart before the horse. I merely copied the Summary from the end of each textbook chapter. Have you ever started a book and skipped to the end for a quick peek at the climax? It is sort of like that. One reason for doing it this way is that you can read the conclusion (the summary) first, and then after you actually study the chapter, you can critique the quality of the authors' summary. Did they do a good job of summarizing the chapter? Did they capture all of the salient elements—the prominent and most remarkable concepts—of the chapter's theme? The number in parentheses is the page in the textbook where you can find the chapter summary.

Key Questions

Each chapter actually opens with an extensive two-four page Field Note based on the author's personal research or experience. In the textbook, the list of Key Questions follows the opening Field Note. I chose to put the Key Questions in this order in the workbook since they represent the primary themes—the highest order in the hierarchical structure of the chapter. Each key question is the same as one of the primary section titles of the main textual part of the textbook. Thus when you look at the Chapter Outline, you will see the Key Questions repeated as section titles.

Field Notes

In addition to an extensive Field Note to open the chapter, there are several other smaller Field Notes interspersed with the primary textual content. Some of these Field Notes are by colleagues and friends (Guest Field Note)—fellow geographers—of the authors. Each of the Field Notes is accompanied by a nice photograph or map relevant to the Field Note. The purpose of the Field Notes is to introduce you to the work of geographers and the wide range of subjects in which human geographers find interest and conduct research.

Thinking Geographically

One of the nice innovations in *Human Geography: People, Place, and Culture* is the "Thinking Geographically" questions placed strategically throughout each chapter. These brief comment-question paragraphs come at the end of each major topical section of the chapter. If you want to see how well you are assimilating the information in the textbook, that is, how closely you are beginning to think about things the way geographers do, read the questions and "think geographically" about your answer. As you contemplate your answer, doodle out little maps and tables and keywords that come to mind. Your ability to answer the question or respond to the comment often requires knowledge not specifically mentioned in the textbook, but will draw on the entire body of knowledge locked away in your brain. In other words, these will help you to do two things that are critical to a successful and fulfilling life: be able to synthesize information, and be able to think critically. This will really help you prepare for the APHG Exam, especially on the free response questions. Your teacher might also be able to use these for classroom activities. I copied the Thinking Geographically paragraphs and page numbers for your quick reference.

Chapter Outline

Finally, I have outlined the textbook chapter for you. Ideally you would have done this yourself **by hand** since it would have given you a pretty good overview of the chapter content, structure and themes. Having preempted that exercise, you have two choices: either 1) look over my outline carefully, or 2) ignore my outline and do your own as I advised in Part One. The part of the chapter I have outlined is the main textual material. In other words, I separated out the ancillary parts of the chapter such as the Key Questions, Field Notes and Thinking Geographically.

Chapter Figures and Tables

I have listed all of the Figures and Tables from each chapter. I give you the figure number, page, type and theme. You never know when you might want to recall a particularly memorable figure, but cannot recollect where in the book you saw it. Maybe these tables will help. I have classified the figures as maps, photos, illustrations, imagery and tables. There is a good chance you are a so-called "visual learner," in which case you will want to develop an intimate relationship with the textbook graphics. I have also chosen one of the figures, either a map or photo or table, and created a little exercise for you under the heading **Exercise for Chapter Figures and Tables**. It is especially important to digest these visual aids since one or more of your APHG Exam Free Response Questions will require interpretation of a map or other graphic element.

Geographic Concepts

Next I have done another cut-and-paste job on the Geographic Concepts, otherwise known as the chapter's vocabulary list or glossary of terms. I am going to take a moment to pontificate—to speak in a pompous way—to make a point, so bear with me. A couple of years ago I saw something in *Time* magazine about the decline of literacy in America. I found a reference by Googling the phrase:

> 14-year-olds in the 1950s knew about 25,000 words, while 14-year-olds today know only about 10,000.

That led me to a URL that is way too long to cite here, but quoting from the article:

> Weeks cites Professor David Orr's commentary from the August 1999 issue of *Conservation Biology*: ". . . the human vocabulary is shrinking. By one reckoning. . . the working vocabulary of 14-year-olds in America has plummeted from 25,000 words in 1950 to 10,000 words today."

Shocking, but not surprising. At lot of cool technology and gadgets—much of it invented by earlier generations—replaced the reading of books for entertainment, television for example, and record players (record what?!). Today we have game boxes and iPods and cell phones with more bells and whistles than a normal person will ever use. The cumulative effect has been the observed decline in our collective ability to use words, which also limits our ability to express complex thoughts.

Some of the words in the Geographic Concepts section at the end of each chapter are a bit jargonistic—the specialized vocabulary and idioms of those in the same profession, in this case geographers. Most of the words, however, are common enough in English, but take on special denotations and connotations in the field of geography. I cannot emphasize enough how important it is for you to master these terms. **On the APHG Exam free response questions, using these terms judiciously—wisely and carefully—and accurately, will enable you to articulate complex ideas with fewness of words, which the Readers (those people scoring your Exam) always appreciate.**

ALERT! That last sentence was crucial. APHG Exam readers DO NOT give points for verbosity. The readers have seen very short essays that used the correct geographic concepts in their proper context, precise and succinct, and therefore received full points. Likewise they have seen long, grammatically well-written essays that simply did not address the question or use the correct terms; ultimately such essays receive few if any points.

All of these terms are defined in the text and in a Glossary at the end of the textbook (Appendix C). Sometimes when I am exposed to a new term, I look for both denotations and nuanced connotations. I admit that I have personally found Wikipedia wickedly useful as a quick first glance, but I also look up terms in specialized on-line glossaries and encyclopedias. A good college dictionary and thesaurus are equally indispensable. When coming upon a word with which you are unfamiliar, it is always worth the effort to stop, look it up, and contemplate how it is used.

Usually there are more than fifteen terms per chapter, but I randomly selected fifteen and created a little matching terms exercise, a **Quiz for Geographic Concepts**, to help reinforce the terms. I have appended an Answer Key at the end of this workbook.

Internet Resources

The next part of the workbook lists the two sections of Internet links that the authors have found relevant to that particular chapter: The links in the **Learn More Online** section tend to be more of the current event and/or informational type website and are drawn from many different sources, such as news media, government and educational institutions, the United Nations, and so on. Those in the **Watch It Online** section seem to be mostly multimedia presentations, primarily from Annenberg Media which is a part of the Annenberg Foundation. These Annenberg video clips are from the series "The Power of Place: Geography for the 21st Century." You will have to register to view the programs on your computer, but registration is free (the Foundation is, after all, a not-for-profit organization). There is also a good chance your school has the complete set on videotape or DVD.

Since "The Power of Place: Geography for the 21st Century" video programs are so widely used in geography education, and since the Annenberg Foundation is such a prominent organization promoting education, I decided to once again cut-and-paste some information from the Internet.

The Annenberg Foundation

Annenberg Foundation
source: http://www.annenbergfoundation.org/about/about_show.htm?doc_id=209617

The Annenberg Foundation is the successor corporation to the Annenberg School at Radnor, Pennsylvania established in 1958 by Walter H. Annenberg. It exists to advance the public well-being through improved communication. As the principal means of achieving its goal, the Foundation encourages the development of more effective ways to share ideas and knowledge.

Ambassador Annenberg has observed that the transmission of information is a factor in every human advancement or reversal. In an age of fiber optic cables and satellites, events are witnessed around the world even as they take place and the very telling of the tale affects the pace and nature of change.

But the revolution wrought by communications began more than five centuries ago. The swift and cheap dissemination of information first made possible by Gutenberg's invention of movable type has given rise to new political, social, and cultural forms that have enhanced life for millions of people.

While the modern computer and broadcast technology are important communications tools, they are only amplifiers and extenders of the visual image, written word, and human voice. The Foundation's focus is not on chips and wires but rather on education, particularly public school restructuring and reform in the United States.   The Foundation is open to collaboration with other philanthropic institutions.

Annenberg Media
source: http://www.learner.org/about/aboutus.html

Annenberg Media uses media and telecommunications to advance excellent teaching in American schools. This mandate is carried out chiefly by the funding and broad distribution of educational video programs with coordinated Web and print materials for the professional development of K-12 teachers. It is part of The Annenberg Foundation and advances the Foundation's goal of encouraging the development of more effective ways to share ideas and knowledge.

Annenberg Media's multimedia resources help teachers increase their expertise in their fields and assist them in improving their teaching methods. Many programs are also intended for

students in the classroom and viewers at home. All Annenberg Media videos exemplify excellent teaching.

The Power of Place: Geography for the 21st Century
source: http://www.learner.org/resources/series180.html

"The Power of Place: Geography for the 21st Century" teaches the geographic skills and concepts that are necessary to understand the world. Geography educators and content experts from around the globe shed light on the physical, human, political, historical, economic, and cultural factors that affect people and natural environments. Maps, animation, and academic commentary bring into focus case studies from 50 sites in 36 countries. Originally produced in 1996, the entire series has been updated. Each case study features new interviews, maps, video footage, and graphics in order to reflect the geographic issues of our world in the 21st century. A coordinated Web site provides further content information and connection to the National Geography Standards.

Produced by Cambridge Studios. 2003.

By the way, **cutting-and-pasting** in a writing project is acceptable as long as you give the proper citation. It is very tempting to cut-and-paste without giving credit to the original source, and that is, of course, a form of cheating we call plagiarism. Don't do it. It is just as easy for teachers to find where you got your information as it was for you to find it and copy it.

In each chapter I choose one of the Watch It Online programs and, naturally, create another exercise for you, **Exercise for Chapter Related Internet Links**, usually asking questions designed to make you think critically and creatively about the information in the program.

APHG-Type Questions

It is somewhat presumptuous of me to call these "APHG-Type Questions" since no one is refereeing the questions I have created or chosen from other sources. In academia, a referee is an academic authority who examines and evaluates an article, book, etc. with regard to its fitness for publication. Questions that make their way to the APHG Exam have literally been evaluated by many very smart people, geographers and professional question writers. One more thing, APHG MC questions always have five possible answers, A through E.

As you read *Human Geography: People, Place, and Culture*, try to think like a teacher. When it comes to assessment—tests, quizzes, projects—consider how the information you are digesting might be framed as multiple choice and free response questions. Take a look at the box below to familiarize yourself with MCQ formats. The examples were drawn from a different academic discipline, however, you will have no problem seeing how different types of questions are conceived and structured. It is safe to say that there is an implied increasing level of difficult with each type of question.

Review of Multiple Choice Question Formats
source: http://www.pepraxis.com/0091/understandmc.htm

Type A: Basic Knowledge. Type A assesses basic knowledge. These questions are factual and simply require the knowledge of a piece of information.

Example:

What most frequently causes a tennis player to miss the ball completely?
A. Swinging too early
B. Swinging too late
C. Not watching the ball
D. Gripping the racket incorrectly

Answer: C

Type B: Application. Type B questions are designed to test basic knowledge and to use it in context. These questions require application of information in a specific context. Such questions do not require the you to address the full complexity of real life situations, but they demand more than simple memorization of facts.

Example:

Billy, at age of two months, is very active and wriggles frequently. The findings of a study on the origins of temperamental or constitutional personality differences would predict that
A. Billy will be very quiet and docile by age 5
B. Billy will succeed in school
C. Billy will very likely be active and unable to sit still for long as a small child
D. Billy will be neurotic

Answer: C

Key words are: "origins of temperamental or constitutional personality differences". This is an example of a question that seems to be a "trick" question. You know that it's going to be more difficult because you not only need to recall some definitions but you need to visualize how they can be applied in real life situations.

Type C: Analysis, Synthesis and Evaluation. Type C questions require that the students analyze, synthesize, evaluate and make a decision. This type of question is based upon a hypothetical situation and asks you to use your knowledge in order to make judgments. These questions often involve a scenario and require integration of knowledge and decision making. Sometimes you must decide the most appropriate steps to take, given a hypothetical case or situation.

Example:

A student suffers an injured an ankle while running to first base in softball game. The teacher questions the student about how the injury occurred and about the area affected. The teacher examines the indicated area. The symptoms are typical of a sprained ankle, although the injury may in fact be more severe. Which of the following steps should be included in the first aid administered to the student?
    I. Elevate the injured leg
   II. Apply ice to the injured area
  III. Apply direct pressure to the site of the injury
        A. I only
        B. II only
        C. I and II only
        D. I and III only

Answer: C

In each of the following chapters of this manual, I try to generate two types of MCQ: the **basic knowledge** kind, and the **application** kind. In my experience, the multiple choice questions on the APHG Exam are only of these two types.

On the other hand, as you saw in Part One, the free response questions DO assume your ability to "analyze, synthesize and evaluate." And not just within the subject matter of a particular chapter. You can expect that one or more of the free response questions on the APHG Exam will require you to synthesize knowledge that must be drawn from two or more chapters. I will attempt just one such question for each chapter, based only on the information in that chapter.

Conclusion

I am sure I have given you a lot to think about. I do not really expect you to do all of the exercises I suggest in this manual. Your teacher will have his or her own ideas about what to do above and beyond reading the textbook. As in all endeavors, the more effort that goes in, the better the outcome. But you have to balance the AP Human Geography work with all of the urgent activities of your life—like sleep, which I do not recommend you sacrifice just to get a top score on the APHG Exam. Find a balance.

And have fun.

CHAPTER 1: INTRODUCTION TO HUMAN GEOGRAPHY

Chapter Summary (34)

Our study of human geography will analyze people and places and explain how they interact across space and time to create our world. Chapters 2 and 3 lay the basis for our study of human geography by looking at where people live. Chapters 4–7 focus on aspects of culture and how people use culture and identity to make sense of themselves in their world. The remaining chapters examine how people have created a world in which they function economically, politically, and socially, and how their activities in those realms re-create themselves and their world.

Key Questions (8)

1.   What is human geography
2.   What are geographic questions?
3.   Why do many geographers use maps, and what do maps tell us?
4.   Why are geographers concerned with scaled and connectedness?
5.   What are geographic concepts, and how are they used in answering geographic questions?

Field Notes

(1-7)   Awakening to World Hunger

(14)   Glacier National Park

(23)   Disease Ecology and GIS

(28)   Montgomery, Alabama (geography of ethnic relations)

Thinking Geographically

(9) Imagine and describe the most remote place on Earth you can think of 100 years ago. Now, describe how globalization has changed this place and how the people there continue to shape it—to make it the place it is today.

(16) Geographers who practice fieldwork keep their eyes open to the world around them and through practice become adept at reading cultural landscapes. Take a walk around your campus or town and try reading the cultural landscape. Choose one thing in the landscape and ask yourself, "What is that and why is it there?" Take the time to find out the answers!

(22) Use Google Earth to find a place where a humanitarian crisis is occurring today (such as Myanmar or Darfur) and study the physical and human geography overlaid on Google Earth in this place. How does studying this place on Google Earth change your mental map of the place and/or your understanding of the crisis?

(32) Once you think about different types of diffusion, you will be tempted to figure out what kind of diffusion is taking place for all sorts of goods, ideas, or diseases. Please remember that any good, idea, or disease can diffuse in more than one way. Choose a good, idea, or disease as an example and describe how it diffused from its hearth across the globe, referring to at least three different types of diffusion.

(33) Choose a geographic concept introduced in this chapter. Think about something that is of personal interest to you (music, literature, politics, science, sports), and think about how you could use a geographic concept to study this interest. Think about space and location, your geographic concept, and your interest. Write a geographic question that could be the foundation of a geographic study.

Chapter Outline

A. What is Human Geography?
B. What Are Geographic Questions?
    1. Maps in the Time of Cholera Pandemics
    2. The Spatial Perspective
        a. The Five Themes
        b. Cultural Landscape
C. Why Do Geographers Use Maps, and What Do Maps Tell Us?
    1. Mental Maps
    2. Generalization in Maps
    3. Remote Sensing and GIS
D. Why Are Geographers Concerned with Scale and Connectedness?
    1. Regions
        a. Perceptual Regions in the United States
    2. Culture
    3. Connectedness Through Diffusion
        a. Expansion Diffusion
        b. Relocation Diffusion
E. What Are Geographic Concepts, and How are They Used in Answering Geographic Questions?
    1. Environmental Determinism
    2. Possibilism
    3. Today's Human Geography

Chapter Figures and Tables

Figure	Page	Type	Theme
1.1	1	photo	Kericho, Kenya tea plantations
1.2	2-3	map	Average Daily Per Capital Calorie Consumption, 2003
1.3	4-5	map	Per Capita Gross National Income (GNI)
1.4	6-7	map	Percent of Land that is Arable (Farmable)
1.5	9	map	Cases of Cholera in the Soho District of London, England, 1854
1.6	10-11	map	Cases of Cholera and Imported Cholera, 2004-2007
1.7	12-13	map	Desirable Places to Live (United States)
1.8	14	photo	Glacier National Park
1.9	15	photo	Mumbai, India and Dar-es-Salaam, Tanzania (apartments)
1.10	17	map	All Roads Lead to Chicago
1.11	18-19	map	Average Annual Precipitation of the World
1.12	20	imagery	Satellite Image of Hurricane Katrina
1.13	21	photo	New Orleans, Louisiana (flooded)
1.14	21	map	The Representation of St. Francis, South Dakota
1.15	23	map	Physical Geography of Hawaii
1.16	24	map	Median Family Income (in U.S. dollars), circa 2006 (No. America)
1.17	25	map	Median Family Income (in U.S. dollars), 2000 (Washington, D.C. area)
1.18	25	photo	Guilin, China (karst)
1.19	27	map	Mid-Atlantic Cultural Region

1.20	27	map	Perceptual Regions of North America
1.21	28	photo	Montgomery, AL Street sign
1.22	30	illustration	Contagious and Hierarchical Diffusion
1.23	31	photos	New Delhi, India McDonalds; Vrindavan, India Sacred Cows

Exercise for Chapter Figures and Tables

As a classroom activity, your teacher can ask your class to look at photos from the chapter, let's say Figure 1.9 on page 15, apartment buildings in Mumbai, India and Dar-es-Salaam, Tanzania. Take a few minutes to digest the visual information. What questions come to mind? Consider the following?

Q. Do the buildings look like standard residential compounds found anywhere in the world, or are there architectural elements that suggest local design?

Q. What do the photos tell us about the mundane tasks of life, such as laundry and parking?

Q. What economic class of people live there? Rich, middle, poor? Would your answer be different if comparing social classes in those countries instead of your instinct to compare them to the United States?

Q. If you were a Peace Corps volunteer, a worker for an international NGO, a missionary, or just someone out for adventure, would you be comfortable living in these buildings? Why or why not?

You can do this same exercise for other figures (maps, photos, illustrations) and tables throughout the book.

Geographic Concepts

Geographic Concepts (Glossary of Terms)		
fieldwork	accessibility	perceptual region
human geography	connectivity	culture
globalization	landscape	culture trait
physical geography	cultural landscape	culture complex
spatial	sequent occupance	cultural hearth
spatial distribution	cartography	independent invention
pattern	reference maps	cultural diffusion
medical geography	thematic maps	time-distance decay
pandemic	absolute location	cultural barrier
epidemic	global positioning system	expansion diffusion
spatial perspective	geocaching	contagious diffusion
five themes	relative location	hierarchical diffusion
location	mental map	stimulation diffusion
location theory	activity space	relocation diffusion
human-environment	generalized map	geographic concept
region	remote sensing	environmental determinism
place	geographic information	isotherm
sense of place	systems	possibilism
perception of place	rescale	cultural ecology
movement	formal region	political ecology
spatial interaction	functional region	
distance		

Quiz for Geographic Concepts

Using the list of geographic concepts, match a term with a definition.

1. _____ cultural ecology

2. _____ human geography

3. _____ location theory

4. _____ remote sensing

5. _____ mental map

6. _____ cultural hearth

7. _____ spatial distribution

8. _____ pandemic

9. _____ cultural landscape

10. _____ thematic maps

11. _____ functional region

12. _____ accessibility

13. _____ contagious diffusion

14. _____ relocation diffusion

15. _____ sense of place

A. Maps that tell stories, typically showing the degree of some attribute or the movement of a geographic phenomenon.

B. A logical attempt to explain the locational pattern of economic activity and the manner in which its producing areas are interrelated.

C. The distance-controlled spreading of an idea, innovation, or some other item through a local population by contact from person to person.

D. The degree of ease with which it is possible to reach a certain location from other locations. It varies from place to place and can be measured.

E. The multiple interactions and relationships between a culture and the natural environment.

F. One of the major divisions of geography; the spatial analysis of human population, its cultures, activities, and landscapes.

G. Physical location of geographic phenomena across space.

H. Image or picture of the way space is organized as determined by an individual's perception, impression, and knowledge of that space.

I. State of mind derived from the infusion of a place with meaning and emotion by remembering important events that occurred in that place or by labeling a place with a certain character.

J. A region defined by that particular set of activities or interactions that occur within it.

K. A method of collecting data or information through the use of instruments that are physically distance from the area or object of study.

L. An outbreak of a disease that spreads worldwide.

M. The visible imprint of human activity and culture on the landscape.

N. Heartland, source area, innovation center; place of origin of a major culture.

O. Sequential diffusion process in which the items being diffused are transmitted by their carrier agents as they evacuate the old area and relocate to new ones.

Internet Resources

Learn More Online

About Careers in Geography
www.aag.org
http://www.bls.gov/opub/ooq/2005/spring/art01.pdf

About Geocaching
www.geocaching.org

About Globalization and Geography
www.lut.ac.uk/gawc/rb/rb40.html

About John Snow and His Work on Cholera
http://www.ph.ucla.edu/epi/snow.html

About the State of Food Insecurity in the World
www.fao.org

About World Hunger
www.wfp.org

About Google Earth
www.googleearth.com

Watch It Online

About Globalization
http:/www.learner.org/resources/series180.html#program_descriptions
click on Video On Demand for "One Earth, Many Scales"

Exercise for Chapter Related Internet Links

Watch the program "One Earth, Many Scales," which is 28 minutes long. Whether as a classroom exercise or on your own at home, think about these questions.

Q. What are some of the main themes?
Q. Were there any parts of the program that were awesome or memorable?
Q. How does the program relate to this chapter in the textbook?

These are very general questions. One popular exercise I use is to show a video program in class, then divide the students into teams of 3-5 students. We then have a quiz show where one team will ask a specific question about the program, and the first other team to raise a hand gets a shot at answering the question. If they get it right, they get a point. When the game is over, I take the average team score and make those points the exercise standard (this is, after all, an evaluated exercise/game). That means that the team(s) with the highest points get some bonus (extra credit) points, while those with the lowest lose some ground. Get incentive to pay attention, don't you think? Of course as teacher I get to be the final arbiter of any disputes, and I also get to make up the rules.

APHG-Type Questions

Note: Be sure to take the online Self Tests on the Student Companion Site.
Check answer key at the end of the workbook.

Multiple Choice Questions

Type A: Basic Knowledge Questions

1. The vast majority of the 1 billion malnourished people are Earth are
   A. soldiers in countries with insurgencies
   B. people above the age of 65
   C. people with chronic diseases such as HIV/AIDS
   D. women and children
   E. girls under the age of 15

2. Until the beginning of the 19th century, cholera was confined to what country(s) or region(s)?
   A. China and Japan
   B. Sub-Saharan Africa
   C. the Amazon Basin
   D. crowded inner-city slums
   E. India

3. Images from a satellite or aerial photos from a plane are both examples of
   A. geographic information systems
   B. map generalization
   C. projection
   D. global positioning
   E. remote sensing

4. A region in which the people share one or more cultural traits.
   A. functional region
   B. perceptual region
   C. formal region
   D. political region
   E. cultural region

5. A combination of cultural traits is a
   A. complex culture
   B. cultural hearth
   C. barrier to diffusion
   D. culture region
   E. cultural complex

6. Hip-hop culture has spread from city to city worldwide in a process of _____ diffusion.
   A. expansion
   B. contagious
   C. stimulus
   D. hierarchical
   E. cultural

7. Latitude and longitude will give you the _____ location of a place.
   A. relative
   B. cultural
   C. reference
   D. situation
   E. absolute

8. All geographers, human or physical, are interested in the _____ of a phenomenon.
   A. spatial distribution
   B. absolute location
   C. diffusion
   D. temporal patterns
   E. origin

9. A set of processes that are increasing interactions and interdependence without regard to country borders.
   A. spatial diffusion
   B. pandemics
   C. globalization
   D. distance decay
   E. accessibility

10. Which of the following is NOT one of the Five Themes of geography?
    A. location
    B. people
    C. human-environment
    D. region
    E. movement

Type B: Application Questions

1. Which of the following is NOT given as a reason contributing to poverty and malnutrition in Kenya?
   A. a globalized economy that thrives on foreign income
   B. a post-colonial vacuum of well-trained economic managers
   C. tiny farms that are unproductive
   D. a gendered legal system that disenfranchises the agricultural labor force
   E. disempowering of the caregivers of the country's children

2. In what ways are the disciplines of geography and history related?
   A. they are equally focused on temporal-spatial phenomena
   B. they are equally focused on spatial-temporal phenomena
   C. within both disciplines, there is consensus on research methodologies
   D. there is significant overlap in their subject matter
   E. the intellectual cores of both are defined by perspectives rather than subject matter

3. "From Mannheim Road, go west on North Avenue till you get to 5th Avenue, then north about ¾ of a mile; it's right next to the water tower." This is an example of
   A. relative location
   B. absolute location
   C. the use of GPS
   D. a mental map
   E. geocaching

4. Different Native American populations in the Southwest evolved different forms of economy, some becoming pastoralists, other sedentary farmers, others hunter-gatherers. This can be explained by which geographic concept?
   A. possibilism
   B. environmental determinism
   C. natural isotherms
   D. expansion diffusion
   E. distance decay

5. Why are you not likely to find an all-beef Big Mac at the McDonalds restaurants in India?
   A. chicken is much cheaper to raise in India
   B. most of the people are Hindus who believe cows are sacred
   C. after the last outbreak of Mad Cow disease, all the cows were slaughtered
   D. all of the people of India are vegetarians
   E. lamb is the preferred red meat in South Asia

Free Response Question

Based on Figure 1.17, Median Family Income (in U.S. dollars), 2000 for the Washington, DC region.

1. What is the areal unit used in this map?
2. Describe the spatial pattern of income distribution in the region.
3. If race is correlated with income in the United States, what does this map say about the distribution of ethnic groups in the region?

CHAPTER 2: POPULATION

Chapter Summary (74)

In the late 1700s, Thomas Malthus sounded warning bells about the rapidly growing population in Great Britain. He feared a massive famine would soon "check" the growing population, bringing widespread suffering. Although the famine in Great Britain did not take place as he predicted, the rapidly growing worldwide population made many more follow Malthus's trajectory, issuing similar warnings about the population explosion over the last two centuries.

The growth rate of the world population has certainly slowed, but human suffering is not over yet. Dozens of countries still face high death rates and high birth rates. Even in countries where the death rate is low, slowed population growth is often a result of horrid sanitary and medical conditions that lead to high infant and child mortality, diseases such as AIDS that ravage the population and orphan the young, or famines that governments deny and that global organizations cannot ameliorate.

Population pyramids illustrate that as wealthier countries worry about supporting their aging populations, poorer countries have problems of their own. A high birth rate in a poor country does not necessarily mean overpopulation—some of the highest population densities in the world are found in wealthy countries. Even poor countries that have lowered their birth rates and their death rates are constantly negotiating what is morally acceptable to their people and their cultures.

Geography offers much to the study of population. Through geography we can see differences in population problems across space, how what happens at one scale affects what goes on at other scales, and how different cultures and countries approach population questions.

Key Questions (39)

1. Where in the world do people live and why?
2. Why do populations rise or fall in particular places?
3. Why does population composition matter?
4. How does the geography of health influence population dynamics?
5. How do governments affect population change?

Field Notes

(36-38) Where Are the Children?

(40)   Crowded Streets of Yangon, Myanmar

(41)   Egyptian Landscapes

(70)   Young Carers in Subsaharan Africa

(71)   Sparrow Rainbow Village, South Africa

Thinking Geographically

(46) As we discussed in the field note at the beginning of this chapter, populations are falling in some parts of the world. How will Figure 2.5 look different 50 years from now? If you were updating this textbook in 50 years, where would the largest population clusters in the world be?

(57) Examine Appendix B at the end of the (text)book. Study the growth rate column. Which countries have the highest growth rates? Determine what stage of the demographic transition these countries are in, and hypothesize what may lead them to the next stage.

(70) Study Figure 2.17, the infant mortality rate (IMR) by state in the United States. Hypothesize why the IMR is low in some regions of the country and high in others. Shift scales in your mind, and take one state and choose one state to consider—how do you think IMR varies within this state—what other factors are involved at this scale and this level of generalization to explain the pattern of IMRs? Use the population Internet sites listed at the end of this chapter to determine whether your hypotheses are correct.

(74) When studying government policies on population, one of the most important things to remember is unintended consequences. Choose one country in the world where women have little access to education and are disempowered. Consider the previous section of this chapter on age composition, and determine how restrictive population policies in this country will alter the population composition of the country.

Chapter Outline

A. Where In The World Do People Live and Why?
  1. Physiologic Population Density
  2. Population Distribution
  3. World Population Distribution and Density
      a. East Asia
      b. South Asia
      c. Europe
      d. North America
  4. Reliability of Population Data
B. Why Do Populations Rise and Fall in Particular Places?
  1. Population Growth at World, Regional, National, and Local Scales
      a. Population Growth at the Regional and National Scales
      b. Population Growth at the Local Scale
  2. The Demographic Transition
  3. Future Population Growth
C. How Does the Geography of Health Influence Population Dynamics?
  1. Infant Mortality
  2. Child Mortality
  3. Life Expectancy
  4. Influence on Health and Well-Being
  5. Infectious Diseases
  6. Chronic and Genetic Diseases
  7. AIDS
E. How Do Governments Affect Population Change?
  1. Limitations
  2. Contradictions

Chapter Figures and Tables

Figure	Page	Type	Theme
2.1	36	photo	Bordeaux, France (street scene)
2.2	38-39	map	Year that Total Fertility Rate Among Women Fell Below Replacement Levels
2.3	40	photo	Yangon, Myanmar Street Scene
2.4	41	photos	Luxor, Egypt (rural scenes)
2.5	42-43	map	World Population Distribution
2.6	44-45	map	World Population Density
2.7	48-49	map	World Population Growth
2.8	50	graph	Population Growth, 1650 to 2050
2.9	51	map	Recent Population Growth Rates in India
2.10	51	photo	Maharashtra, India (family planning)
2.11	52-53	map	Crude Birth Rate: Number of Births in a Year per 1,000 People
2.12	54-55	map	Crude Death Rate: Number of Deaths in a Year per 1,000 People
2.13	56	graph	The Demographic Transition Model
2.14	58	graph	Age-Sex Population Pyramids for Countries with High Population Growth Rates
2.15	58	graph	Age-Sex Population Pyramids for Countries with Low Population Growth Rates
2.16	60-61	map	Infant Mortality Rate, 2007
2.17	62	map	Infant Mortality Rate in the United States
2.18	64-65	map	2008 Mothers' Index Rankings
2.19	66-67	map	Life Expectancy at Birth in Years
T2.1	68	table	Leading Causes of Death in the United States, 2005
2.20	69	graph	Affect of AIDS on the Population Pyramid for South Africa, predicted 2035
2.21	71	photo	Sparrow Rainbow Village, Johannesburg, South Africa
2.22	70	illustration	Drawing by a boy from North Western Kenya
2.23	72	photo	Chengdu, China (one-child policy billboard)
2.24	73	graph	China Population Pyramid
2.25	73	graph	Aging Population of China

Exercise for Chapter Figures and Tables

Compare Figure 2.5 World Population Distribution (page 42-43) and Figure 2.6 World Population Density (page 44-45).

- What is the main theme of both maps?
- How are these maps different?
- What are the advantages and/or disadvantages of the two designs?

Geographic Concepts

Geographic Concepts (Glossary of Terms)		
population density	crude birth rate	chronic or degenerative diseases
arithmetic population density	crude death rate	
physiological population density	demographic transition	genetic or inherited diseases
	stationary population level	endemic AIDS
population distribution	population composition	expansive population policies
dot map	population pyramids	eugenic population policies
megalopolis	infant mortality rate	restrictive population policies

census	newborn mortality rate	one-child policies
doubling time	child mortality rate	
population explosion	life expectancy	
natural increase	infectious diseases	

Quiz for Geographic Concepts

Using the list of geographic concepts, match a term with a definition.

1. ____ population pyramid

2. ____ chronic or degenerative diseases

3. ____ population density

4. ____ dot map

5. ____ life expectancy

6. ____ population explosion

7. ____ megalopolis

8. ____ crude birth rate

9. ____ child mortality rate

10. ____ population composition

11. ____ demographic transition

12. ____ doubling time

13. ____ physiological population density

14. ____ eugenic population policies

15. ____ natural increase

A. Population growth measured as the excess of live births over deaths. Does not reflect either emigrant or immigrant movements.

B. The number of live births yearly per thousand people in a population.

C. Structure of a population in terms of age, sex and other properties such as marital status and education.

D. A measurement of the number of people per given unit of land.

E. A figure indicating how long, on average, a person may be expected to live.

F. The time required for a population to double in size.

G. The rapid growth of the world's human population during the past century, attended by ever-shortening doubling times and accelerating rates of increase.

H. Used to designate large coalescing supercities that are forming in diverse parts of the world.

I. Visual representation of the age and sex composition of a population whereby the percentage of each group (generally five-year increments) is represented by a horizontal bar the length of which represents its relationship to the total population.

J. Generally long-lasting afflictions now more common because of higher life expectancies.

K. Government policies designed to favor one racial sector over others.

L. The number of people per unit area of arable land.

M. Multistage model of changes in population growth exhibited by countries undergoing industrialization.

N.   Map where one dot represents a certain number of a phenomenon, such as a population.

O.   Describes the number of children that die between the first and fifth years of their lives in a given population.

Chapter Related Internet Links

Learn More Online

About Population Growth in the World
http://www.prb.org

About the Composition of the Population of the United States
http://www.census.gov

About the Global AIDS Crisis
http://www.unaids.org/en

About International Population Programs
http://www.unfpa.org

Watch It Online

About the Population Transition in Italy
http://www.learner.org/resources/series85.html#program_descriptions
click on Video On Demand for "Population Transition in Italy"

Exercises for Chapter Related Internet Links

Watch the program "Population Transition in Italy."

- What is the demographic phenomenon that is being discussed?
- After watching the program at home (or in class), have your teacher organize a debate on the issue.
- As an exercise, and to help you think critically about the subject, you can create a table with two columns, one for the benefits derived from the issue being discussed, and one for the negative consequences.
- Decide how you personally feel about this population trend.
- Is the same phenomenon apparent in the United States? If not, how do U.S. population trends differ from Italy's?

Note: Be sure to take the online Self Tests on the Student Companion Site.
Check answer key at the end of the workbook.

Multiple Choice Questions

Type A: Basic Knowledge.

1. Which of the following is NOT a component of population growth?
   A. crude birth rate
   B. crude death rate
   C. immigration
   D. total fertility rate
   E. emigration

2. Which of the following statements about Europe's population trends is true?
   A. Italy, a Catholic country, has the highest total fertility rate
   B. Sweden has been trying to reduce its population growth rate
   C. Ireland initiated a guns for sterilization exchange campaign in the 1970s
   D. England is in stage 3 of the demographic transition model
   E. not a single country in Europe is above the replacement level

3. An index that relates a country's population density to its available arable land.
   A. physiologic density
   B. population density
   C. arithmetic density
   D. distribution density
   E. crop density

4. Region of the world with the largest population density.
   A. South Asia
   B. Europe
   C. Eastern North America
   D. Eastern coastal South America
   E. East Asia

5. What is the world's population based on the number in the textbook?
   A. 5.4 million
   B. 5.4 billion
   C. 6.4 million
   D. 6.4 billion
   E. 7.4 million

6. Which of the following statements is true?
   A. the slowest growing countries are in the economically wealthier area
   B. the slowest growing countries are in the economically poorer area
   C. the fastest growing countries are in southern Africa
   D. Russia's population is in decline because of its one-child policy
   E. China family planning programs once included guns exchanged for sterilization

7. In what two stages of the demographic transition model does population grow rapidly?
   A. stages 1 & 2
   B. stages 2 & 3
   C. stages 3 & 4
   D. stages 1 & 4
   E. stages 4 & 5

8. Which of the following is NOT directly indicated on a population pyramid?
   A. % of population
   B. life expectancy
   C. age cohorts in five-year increments
   D. males
   E. females

9. What country has the highest life expectancies in the world?
   A. United States
   B. Canada
   C. Sweden
   D. France
   E. Japan

10. Where in the world has the AIDS epidemic had the greatest impact?
    A. inner-city United States
    B. Russia
    C. Subsaharan Africa
    D. Southeast Asia
    E. southwest China

Type B: Application.

1. Population data reported by different agencies—such as the UN, World Bank, and the Population Reference Bureau—are often inconsistent. Why is that?
   A. these use different sampling techniques
   B. reported demographic figures are often estimates rather than actual counts
   C. the different agencies count the population at different times
   D. some of these agencies have better statisticians than others
   E. none of them are doing primary research, their data comes from national governments

2. In countries where cultural traditions restrict educational and professional opportunities for women, and men dominate as a matter of custom, what is the usual impact on population growth rates?
   A. rates of natural increase tend to be high
   B. rates of natural increase tend to be low
   C. total fertility rates tend to be low
   D. infant mortality tends to be high
   E. there is no discernible correlation

3. Which of the following is a consequence of Sweden's policies to encourage more children per family?
    A. more children then means more workers now, so guest workers not getting visas
    B. the government had to switch to more restrictive population policies
    C. not enough government funds to care for the boom generation in their old age
    D. more single women started having children out of marriage
    E. the brief increase in children in 1991 required new classrooms for the temporary population boom

4. According to UN calculations in 2003, how much was needed to combat AIDS worldwide, and how much was available?
    A. $20 billion needed, $5 billion available
    B. $10 billion needed, $5 billion available
    C. $5 billion needed, $1 billion available
    D. $40 billion needed, $15 billion available
    E. $30 billion needed, $10 billion available

5. In what way does a famine limit population growth?
    A. famine is caused by changes in climate that make it difficult for crops plants to adjust
    B. less food available for families, so fertility rates decline
    C. non-democratic governments often use famine as an excuse to implement eugenic population policies
    D. famines are caused by overpopulation, so there is a natural self-regulating mechanism to leads to slower population growth
    E. decreased food consumption leads to weakening of immune systems making people more susceptible to disease

Free Response Question

The Rostow model of economic development postulates that economic modernization occurs in five basic stages:
    1. Traditional society (pre-scientific understanding of gadgets)
    2. Preconditions for take-off (secular education, capital mobilization, entrepreneurial class)
    3. Take-off (society drive by economic processes rather than tradition)
    4. Drive to maturity (economy diversifies, poverty decreases, rising standards of living)
    5. Age of high mass consumption (consumers concentrate on durable goods)

The demographic transition model (DTM) in Figure 2.13 postulates four stages.

1. If you were to add a fifth stage to the demographic transition model, how would you label it in terms of population growth? What would be the characteristics of a fifth stage

2. If you were to correlate the five stages of the Rostow model with the revised five stages of the DTM, what would you be able to hypothesize or conclude?

CHAPTER 3: MIGRATION

Chapter Summary (108)

In the last 500 years, humans have traveled the globe, mapped it, connected it through globalization, and migrated across it. In this chapter, we discussed major global, regional, and national migration flows. Migration can occur as a result of a conscious decision, resulting in a voluntary migration flow, or migration can occur under duress, resulting in forced migration. Both kinds of migration have left an indelible mark on the world and on its cultural landscapes. Governments attempt to strike a balance among the need for migrant labor, the desire to help people in desperate circumstances, and the desire to stem the tide of migration.

As the world's population mushrooms, the volume of migrants will expand. In an increasingly open and interconnected world, neither physical barriers nor politically motivated legislation will stem tides that are as old as human history. Migrations will also further complicate an already complex global cultural pattern—raising questions about identity, race, ethnicity, language, and religion, the topics we turn to in the next three chapters.

Key Questions

1. What is migration?
2. Why do people migrate?
3. Where do people migrate?
4. How do governments affect migration?

Field Notes

(76-79) Risking Lives for Remittances

(87)   Volcano damage, Montserrat

(95)   Israeli settlements in the West Bank

Thinking Geographically

(82) Choose one type of cyclic or periodic movement and then think of a specific example of the kind of movement you chose. Now, determine how this movement changes both the home and the destination. How do these places change as a result of this cyclic or period movement?

(88) Think about a migration flow within your family, whether internal, international, voluntary, or forced. The flow can be one you experienced or one you only heard about through family. List the push and pull factors. Then, write a letter in the first person (if you were not involved, pretend you were your grandmother or whomever) to another family member at "home" describing how you came to migrate to the destination.

(103) Imagine you are from an extremely poor country, and you earn less than $1 a day. Choose a country to be from, and look for it on a map. Assume you are a voluntarily migrant. You look at your access to transportation and the opportunities you have to go elsewhere. Be realistic, and describe how you determine where you will go, how you get there, and what you do once you get there.

(105) One goal of international organizations involved in aiding refugees is repatriation—return of the refugees to their home countries once the threat against them has passed. Take the example of Sudanese refugees. Think about how their land and their lives have changed since they became refugees. You are assigned the daunting task of repatriating Sudanese from Uganda once a peace solution is reached. What steps would you have to take to re-discover a home for these refugees?

Chapter Outline

A. What is Migration?
   1. Cyclic Movement
   2. Periodic Movement
   3. Migration
B. Why Do People Migrate?
   1. Forced Migration
   2. Push and Pull Factors in Voluntary Migration
   3. Types of Push and Pull Factors
      a. Legal Status
      b. Economic Conditions
      c. Power Relationships
      d. Political Circumstances
      e. Armed Conflict and Civil War
      f. Environmental Conditions
      g. Culture and Traditions
      h. Technological Advances
C. Where Do People Migrate?
   1. Global Migration Flows
   2. Regional Migration Flows
      a. Economic Opportunities
      b. Reconnection of Cultural Groups
      c. Conflict and War
   3. National Migration Flows
   4. Guest Workers
   5. Refugees
      Regions of Dislocation
         Sub-Saharan Africa
         North Africa and Southwest Asia
         South Asia
         Southeast Asia
         Europe
         Other Regions
D. How Do Governments Affect Migration?
   1. Legal Restrictions
   2. Waves of Immigration in the United States
   3. Post-September 11

Chapter Figures and Tables

Figure	Page	Type	Theme
3.1	76	photo	Miami Florida (Haitians off the Florida coast)
3.2	78	map	Legal Immigration from Middle and South America to the United States, 1981-2002
3.3	79	photo	Tijuana, Mexico (border wall)
3.4	81	map	Recent Internal Migration in the United States
3.5	83	map	The Atlantic Slave Trade
3.6	85	graph	Distance Decay
3.7	87	photo	Sourfriere Hills, Montserrat (volcano damage)
3.8	90-91	map	Major Routes of Human Migrations before 1950
3.9	92	map	Islands of Development in Sub-Saharan Africa
3.10	93	map	Chinese in Southeast Asia
3.11	94	map	Changing Boundaries of Israel
3.12	95	photo	Jerusalem, Israel (West Bank settlement)
3.13	95	map	Changing Center of Population (United States)
3.14	98	photo	(pending)
3.15	100-101	map	Average Refugee Population between 1994-2003 by Country of Origin
3.16	102	photo	(pending, Crisis in Darfur)
3.17	104	graph	Immigration to the United States by Region, 1820 to 2001
3.18	106-107	map	Countries from which Asylum Seekers to the United States are Automatically Detained

Exercises for Chapter Figures and Tables

Look at Figure 3.18, Countries from which Asylum Seekers to the United States are Automatically Detained.
- What do these countries have in common?
- How are these countries different?
- What might be reasons for asylum seekers from these countries to be detained?
- Do you agree with the policy that they be automatically detained? Why?

Geographic Concepts

Geographic Concepts (Glossary of Terms)		
remittances	laws of migration	regional scale
cyclic movements	gravity model	islands of development
periodic movement	push factors	guest workers
migration	pull factors	refugees
activity spaces	distance decay	internally displaced
nomadism	step migration	persons
migrant labor	intervening opportunity	asylum
transhumance	deportation	repatriation
military service	kinship links	genocide
international migration	chain migration	immigration laws
immigration	immigration wave	quotas
internal migration	global-scale migration	selective immigration
forced migration	explorers	
voluntary migration	colonization	

48

Quiz for Geographic Concepts

Match the term with the definition.

1. ____ chain migration

2. ____ forced migration

3. ____ pull factors

4. ____ colonization

5. ____ asylum

6. ____ distance decay

7. ____ remittances

8. ____ nomadism

9. ____ migrant labor

10. ____ gravity model

11. ____ intervening opportunity

12. ____ international refugees

13. ____ islands of development

14. ____ selective migration

15. ____ laws of migration

A. Physical process whereby the colonizer takes over another place, putting its own government in charge and either moving its own people into the place, or bringing in indentured outsiders to gain control of the people and the land.

B. Positive conditions and factors that effectively attract people to new locales from other areas.

C. Refugees who have crossed one or more international boundaries during their dislocation, searching for asylum in a different country.

D. Movement among a definite set of places—often cyclic movement.

E. A common type of periodic movement involving millions of workers in the United States and tens of millions of workers worldwide who cross international borders in search of employment.

F. Developed by British demographer Ernst Ravenstein, conditions that predict the flow of migrants.

G. Process to control immigration in which individuals with certain backgrounds are barred from immigrating.

H. Place built up by a government or corporation to attract foreign investment and which has relatively high concentrations of paying jobs and infrastructure.

I. Pattern of migration that develops when migrants move along and through kinship links.

J. The effects of distance on interaction, generally the greater the distance the less the interaction.

K. Human migration flows in which the movers have no choice but to relocate.

L. The presence of a nearer opportunity that greatly diminishes the attractiveness of sites further away.

M. Money migrants send back to family and friends in their home countries, often in cash, forming an important part of the economy in many poorer countries.

N.   Shelter and protection in one state for refugees from another state.

O.   A mathematical prediction of the interaction of places, the interaction being a function of the population size of the respective places and the distance between them.

Chapter Related Internet Links

Learn More Online

About Immigration to the United States
http://www.uscis.gov

About Refugees
http://www.unhcr.ch

About Geographic Mobility and Movement in the United States
http://www.census.gov/population/www/socdemo/migrate.html

Watch It Online

About Migration and Identity
http://www.learner.org/resources/series85.html#program_descriptions
click on Video On Demand for "A Migrants Heart"

About the United States-Mexico Border Region
http://www.learner.org/resources/series180.html#program_descriptions
click on Video On Demand for "Boundaries and Borderlands"

Exercise for Chapter Related Internet Links

Watch the program "Borderlands and Boundaries" (28 min 41 sec).

- What are the four geographic themes highlighted in this program? Discuss their definitions and their relevance to this program.
- What is a maquiladora? Discuss this phenomenon in terms of geographic themes.
- Compare and discuss formal employment in a maquiladora with the informal activity of daily smuggling across the US-Mexico border.
- Discuss the various kinds of "region" mentioned in the program.
- What is the name of the woman highlighted in the program? Discuss her life and family in two ways: as real people, and as a statistic.
- What is "Hold the Line," and what are its consequences?
- Have a debate on the Mexican immigration issue.

Note: Be sure to take the online Self Tests on the Student Companion Site.
Check answer key at the end of the workbook.

Multiple Choice Questions

Type A: Basic Knowledge.

1. The name for the seasonal migration of farmers and their cattle up and down the mountain slopes of Switzerland?
   A. internal migration
   B. commuting
   C. activity spaces
   D. transhumance
   E. voluntary migration

2. On average, about how often does the average American citizen move?
   A. 4 years
   B. 5 years
   C. 6 years
   D. 7 years
   E. 8 years

3. On what African island was the East African slave trade concentrated?
   A. Zanzibar
   B. Madagascar
   C. Mayotte
   D. Comoros
   E. Mauritius

4. In mathematical terms, it is the multiplication of the populations of two places divided by the distance between them.
   A. law of migration
   B. intervening opportunity
   C. push-pull equation
   D. transhumance
   E. gravity model

5. What Southeast Asian people were brought by the Dutch to settle their colony of Suriname (Dutch Guiana)?
   A. Javanese
   B. Malaysians
   C. Singaporeans
   D. Sumatrans
   E. Filipinos

6. What minority group in Southeast Asia accounts for 14% of the Thailand, 32 % of the Malaysia, and 76% of the Singapore populations?
   A. Tamil Indians
   B. Chinese
   C. Sri Lankans
   D. Filipinos
   E. Burmese

7. Russification refers to
   A. the evolution of the Rus from their Scandinavian origins (the Varangians) to the Eastern Slavs
   B. the adoption of the russet potato as the staple of the Irish diet
   C. a Soviet era restrictive immigration policy
   D. the return of Russians to Russia after the dissolution of the Soviet Union
   E. Russia's policy to encourage Russians to migrate to non-Russian parts of their land empire

8. Civil wars have recently been fought in what two West African countries?
   A. Guinea and Senegal
   B. Guinea and Ivory Coast
   C. Liberia and Sierra Leone
   D. Gambia and Ghana
   E. Nigeria and Cameroon

9. Why did the United States restrict immigration from Southern Europe after WWI?
   A. many white Americans saw the darker skinned Southern Europeans as an inferior race of whites
   B. the region was a hotbed of anti-Americanism
   C. Southern Europe was technologically less sophisticated
   D. at the time, the U.S. was favoring immigrants from China to work on the railroads
   E. on the contrary, Southern European immigration accelerated after WWI

10. Where is the worst refugee crisis in the world today?
    A. Sudan
    B. Nigeria
    C. Rwanda-Burundi
    D. Palestine
    E. Cambodia

Type B: Application.

1. Why are there such large numbers of Kurdish refugees in the Middle East?
   A. long-term drought has forced them off their lands
   B. Turkey is the only country that accepts Kurds as refugees
   C. Kurds are ethnically related to the Roma (Gypsies) and are not welcome in most countries
   D. a consequence of the US invasion of Iraq
   E. the Kurds are a nation (an ethnic group) without a sovereign state of their own

2. Which of the following is an example of chain migration?
   A. drought leads to famine in the Punjab, which leads to desperation, which leads to emigration
   B. the Dutch first brought people from Indonesia to the Caribbean, and then from other Dutch colonies around the world
   C. one village after another comes under attack by rebels, forcing the people of those villages to migrate to safer areas
   D. in a rural town in Jalisco, Mexico, one person manages to migrate legally to the United States and settles in Elgin, Illinois. He finds a job, prospers, and writes home of his success. Ten years later there is a community of 350 people from Jalisco living in Elgin.
   E. refers specifically to migrations from Central America, starting in Mexico, then moving through the Central American states of Guatemala, Belize, Honduras, Nicaragua, El Salvador, Costa Rica, and finally Panama

3. Which of the following was NOT given as a reason for the disparity between the UN's calculation of global refugees, and the numbers given by other organizations?
   A. the UN inflates the numbers thus requiring a bigger budget to provide aid to refugees
   B. different definitions for what constitutes a refugee
   C. refugees often flee to remote areas where they cannot be counted
   D. governments sometimes manipulate refugees numbers for political reasons
   E. the distinction between internal and international refugees

4. Which of the following is a consequence of the large number of men who died in both World Wars?
   A. large numbers of North Africans (e.g., Algerians) migrated to German-speaking countries
   B. after the war, women replaced men in factory jobs
   C. Germany, in particular, brought in guest workers, mainly from Turkey
   D. most European countries adopted restrictive immigration policies
   E. the center of European population shifted to the southeast

5. What is one of the consequences of the fences the US builds along the border with Mexico, especially those separating cities on both sides of the border?
   A. since the fences are designed to be attractive and friendly, relations between the countries have improved
   B. US companies are investing more in maquiladoras
   C. desperate migrants have started carrying guns and confronting the Border Patrol
   D. remittances from the US to Mexico have been sharply reduced
   E. it forces illegal immigrants to cross in hostile terrain, such as deserts, leading to more people dying

Free Response Questions

Define push and pull factors. Give three generic examples of each. Give one specific example of a global migration flow from one country to the United States, and apply the push-pull factor concept to explain that flow.

CHAPTER 4: LOCAL CULTURE, POPULAR CULTURE, AND CULTURAL LANDSCAPES

Chapter Summary (from page 137)

Advances in transportation and communications technology help popular culture diffuse at record speeds around the world today. Popular culture changes quickly, offering new music, foods, fashions, and sports. Popular culture envelopes and infiltrates local cultures, presenting constant challenges to members of local cultures. Some members of local cultures have accepted popular culture, others have rejected it, and still others have forged a balance between the two.

Customs from local cultures are often commodified, propelling them into popular culture. The search for an "authentic" local culture custom generally ends up promoting a stereotyped local culture or glorifying a single aspect of that local culture. Local culture, like popular culture, is dynamic, and the pursuit of authenticity disregards the complexity and fluidity cultures.

Key Questions

1. What are local and popular cultures?
2. How are local cultures sustained?
3. How is popular culture diffused?
4. How can local and popular cultures be seen in the cultural landscape?

Field Notes

(110-111)   Preserving Culture

(118)   Lindsborg, Kansas and Swedish culture

(119)   New York's ethnic neighborhoods

(124)   The Dingle Peninsula of Ireland

Thinking Geographically

(113) Employing the concept of hierarchical diffusion, describe how you became a "knower" of your favorite kind of music—where is its hearth, and how did it reach you?

(124) What is the last place you went to or the last product you purchased that claimed to be "authentic?" What are the challenges of defending the authenticity of this place or product while refuting the authenticity of other similar places or products?

(131) Think about your local community (your college campus, your neighborhood, or your town). Determine how your local community takes one aspect of popular culture and makes it your own.

(137) Focus on the cultural landscape of your college campus. Think about the concept of placelessness. Determine whether your campus is a "placeless place" or if the cultural landscape of your college reflects the unique identity of the place. Imagine you are hired to build a new student union on your campus. How could you design the building to reflect the uniqueness of your college?

Chapter Outline

A. What Are Local and Popular Cultures?
B. How Are Local Cultures Sustained?
    1.   Rural Local Cultures
        a. The Makah American Indians
        b. Little Sweden, USA
    2.   Urban Local Cultures
    3.   Local Cultures and Cultural Adaptation
    4.   Authenticity of Places
        Guinness and the Irish Pub Company
C. How Is Popular Culture Diffused?
    1.   Hearths of Popular Culture
        a. Establishing a Hearth
        b. Manufacturing a Hearth
           Reterritorialization of Hip Hop
    2.   Replacing Old Hearth with New: Beating Out the Big Three in Popular Sports
    3.   Stemming the Tide of Popular Culture—Losing the Local?
D. How Can Local and Popular Cultures Be seen in the Cultural Landscape?
    Cultural Landscapes of Local Cultures

Chapter Figures and Tables

Figure	Page	Type	Theme
4.1	110	photo	Tata building, Hyderabad, India
4.2	113	photo	Sarah Jessica Parker
4.3	113	photo	Ashton Kucher with Kabbalah bracelet
4.4	115	photo	A Hutterite boy near Stratford, South Dakota
4.5	116	map	Hutterite Colonies in North America
4.6	117	photo	Neah Bay, Washington. Makkah American Indians
4.7	118	photo	Lindsborg, Kansas (Little Sweden, USA)
4.8	119	photo	Williamsburg, Brooklyn, New York (Hasidic Jews & marathoners)
4.9	121	map	Sun City, South Africa (Lost City Resort)
4.10	121	photo	Irish Pub Company designed pub in Dubai
4.11	122-123	maps	Irish Pubs Designed by the Irish Pub Company
4.12	124	photo	Dingle, Ireland
4.13	125	models	Distance Decay and Time Space Compression
4.14	126	photo	Dave Matthews Band
4.15	126	map	Dave Matthews Band concert venues
4.16	127	photo	MTV Studios, Times Square, New York
4.17	129	photo	Professional skateboarder Tony Hawk
4.18	130	photo	Chuck "The Iceman" Liddell, ultimate fighter
4.19	131	photo	Roseville, Minnesota, fast food restaurants
4.20	132-133	map	World Distribution of Skyscrapers
4.21	134	photo	Taipei 101 skyscraper, Taipei, Taiwan
4.22	134	photo	Hard Rock Café, Munich, Germany
4.23	135	photos	Venice, Italy; Venetian Hotel, Las Vegas; Venetian Hotel, Macao
4.24	136	map	Mormon Cultural Region, North America
4.25	137	photo	Traditional Mormon landscape

Exercise for Chapter Figures and Tables

Look at Figure 4.20, World Distribution of Skyscrapers. Compare this to the list of 100 tallest buildings in the world at:

http://www.infoplease.com/ipa/A0001338.html

Photocopy Figure 4.20 and place dots for the locations of any buildings not on the above list, or use a classroom map and mark the location of all one hundred buildings.

- Discuss why the location of skyscrapers is relevant to a chapter on culture.
- Consider other reasons for the spatial pattern of skyscrapers including economic, political or cultural factors that account for the distribution.
- What challenges do these ever-higher buildings pose for the flow of people in and out of the CBD (central business district)?

Geographic Concepts

Geographic Concepts (Glossary of Terms)		
culture	assimilation	time–space compression
folk culture	custom	reterritorialization
popular culture	cultural appropriation	cultural landscape
local culture	neolocalism	placelessness
material culture	ethnic neighborhood	global-local continuum
nonmaterial culture	commodification	glocalization
hierarchical diffusion	authenticity	folk-housing regions
hearth	distance decay	diffusion routes

Quiz for Geographic Concepts

Match the term with the definition.

1. ____ diffusion routes

2. ____ assimilation

3. ____ distance decay

4. ____ time-space compression

5. ____ culture

6. ____ hearth

7. ____ glocalization

8. ____ nonmaterial culture

9. ____ commodification

A. Cultural traits such as dress, diet, and music that identify and are part of today's changeable, urban-based, media-influenced western societies.

B. The process by which cultures adopt customs and knowledge from other cultures and use them for their own benefit.

C. The spatial trajectory through which cultural traits or other phenomena spread.

D. The area where an idea or cultural trait originates.

E. Refers to the social and psychological effects of living in a world in which time-space convergence has rapidly reached a high level of intensity.

F. The seeking out of the regional culture and reinvigoration of it in response to the uncertainty of the modern world.

10. ____ neolocalism

11. ____ global local
    continuum

12. ____ folk culture

13. ____ cultural
    appropriation

14. ____ cultural landscape

15. ____ popular culture

G. The notion that what happens at the global scale has a direct effect on what happens at the local scale, and vice versa.

H. The effects of distance on interaction, generally the greater the distance the less the interaction.

I. Cultural traits such as dress modes, dwellings, traditions, and institutions of usually small, traditional communities.

J. The process through which something is given monetary value; occurs when a good or an idea that previously was not regarded as an object to be bought and sold is turned into something that has a particular price.

K. The expansion of economic, political, and cultural processes to the point that they become global in scale and impact.

L. The sum total of the knowledge, attitudes, and habitual behavioral patterns shared and transmitted by the members of a society.

M. The visible imprint of human activity and culture on the landscape.

N. The beliefs, practices, aesthetics, and values of a group of people.

O. The process through which people lose originally differentiating traits, such as dress and speech, when they come into contact with another society or culture.

Chapter Related Internet Links

Learn More Online

About the Irish Pub Company
http://www.irishpubcompany.com

About the Makah Tribe
http://www.makah.com

About the City of Lindsborg
http://www.lindsborg.org

About the Hutterites
http://www.hutterites.org

About the Religious Societies of the North End
http://www.northendboston.org

Merchants of Cool
http://www.pbs.org/wgbh/pages/frontline/shows/cool/

The Way the Music Died
http://www.pbs.org/wgbh/pages/frontline/shows/music

Exercise for Chapter Related Internet Links

Go to the PBS/Frontline website for information on the special report: "Merchants of Cool."
Watch the entire program and/or read all of the information.
- Do you agree with their findings about teen pop culture?
- How do you "feel" about their research? Is it "real?"
- Talk to your teachers and your parents about what was "cool" in their day, and discuss those differences in terms of similarities and dissimilarities, and available technologies.

APHG-Type Questions

Note: Be sure to take the online Self Tests on the Student Companion Site.
Check answer key at the end of the workbook.

Multiple Choice Questions

Type A: Basic Knowledge.

1. How do the Hutterites differ from the Amish?
   A. Hutterites wear clothing that is less traditional than the Amish
   B. the Amish wear clothing that is less traditional than the Hutterites
   C. Hutterite children will attend regular public schools
   D. Hutterites readily accept technologies that help their agricultural work
   E. the Amish readily accept technologies that help their agricultural work

2. Which of the following statements about St. Patrick's Day is true?
   A. it transcends ethnicity to be celebrated as part of popular culture
   B. the traditional red colors of St. Patrick's Day represents the blood of Irish Catholic martyrs
   C. Protestant Christians generally eschew St. Patrick's Day festivities
   D. the parade is a form of urban local culture
   E. it is customary for women in the parade to wear a corset bodice dress

3. What are the two goals of local cultures?
   A. commodification of their material and nonmaterial culture
   B. escape persecution and find a place to practice their religion
   C. preserve tradition and assimilate with local residents
   D. appropriate the customs of other cultures and make it authentically their own
   E. keep other cultures out and keep their own culture in

4. What aspect of traditional Makah American Indian culture are the Makah trying to revive in order to return to their cultural roots?
   A. the bison hunt
   B. planting the variety of corn cultivated in the 1800s
   C. the whale hunt
   D. building dwellings that reflect the styles and materials of their ancestors
   E. a sport that resembles a cross between modern soccer and lacrosse

5. What is the greatest challenge to urban local cultures?
   A. migration of "others" into their neighborhoods
   B. deterioration of housing stock
   C. discrimination by the mainstream culture
   D. dissemination of popular culture through media
   E. a younger generation not interested in the old ways

6. The rapid diffusion of innovations through modern technology that quickly links distant locations.
   A. distance decay
   B. authenticity transmission
   C. reterritorialization
   D. time-space compression
   E. placelessness

7. The common American house type known as the "ranch" style
   A. is a variation of the New England style
   B. was designed to efficiently use retain heat
   C. originated in the West and diffused eastward
   D. usually has two stories
   E. resembles the saltboxes of the 19th century

8. What was the policy by which the U.S. government tried to make Native Americans more like the Americans of European (white) descent?
   A. cultural appropriation
   B. ethnic reformation
   C. neolocalism
   D. assimilation
   E. commodification

9. Distance decay ensures that
   A. the quality of an innovation decreases with distance from its hearth
   B. obstacles to the diffusion of a cultural innovation, such as music or fashion
   C. better connected cities, regardless of distance, will receive innovations quicker than nearby but less connected locations
   D. the decreasing authenticity of a cultural trait as it diffuses globally
   E. a cultural innovation, once it diffuses widely, cannot be traced back to its original hearth

10. What sport did Tony Hawk help to popularize and become mainstream?
    A. soccer
    B. extreme yodeling
    C. motocross
    D. hang gliding
    E. skateboarding

Type B: Application.

1. These kids in Katmandu, Nepal wear the styles and listen to the music of Hip Hop culture, but with Nepalese accents. This type of diffusion is called
   A. hearth diffusion
   B. relocation
   C. phishing
   D. contagious diffusion
   E. reterritorialization

2. Which of the following is an example of cultural appropriation?
   A. extreme sports becoming mainstream sports
   B. Japan's adoption of Western technology in the late 1800s, but not the West's cultural values
   C. an American rural community descended from Germans deciding to have an annual German festival
   D. celebrities adopting some aspect of a local culture, resulting in that local culture becoming more accessible to popular culture trends
   E. the homogenization of the world's cultural landscape (McDonaldization)

3. Which of the following might best explain the current clash of Eastern and Western civilizations?
   A. jealousy over the material disparities
   B. the resistance Western cultures have to the diffusion of Eastern cultural traits
   C. the geopolitics of petroleum production and consumption
   D. a clash of cultures as Eastern cultures fear the spread of materialistic Western values
   E. frustration in the East over Western immigration policies

4. The creation or distribution of products or services intended for a global or transregional market, but customized to suit local laws or culture.
   A. hierarchical diffusion
   B. manufactured hearth
   C. authentification
   D. commodification
   E. glocalization

5. Which of the following would be an example of commodification?
   A. a person trying to sell their autobiography, after the rights to their story is bought and marketed by a publisher
   B. Native Americans using Chinese factories to manufacture traditional products so that they can be sold to the mass market
   C. souvenir coffee cups and other bric-a-brac sold at tourist traps
   D. the phenomenon of Cabbage Patch dolls in the 1980s which were meant to be a mass market toy but became collectors items which people traded at values well above the original purchase price
   E. after China started reforming its economy in the 1980s, "dormitories," i.e., housing provided nearly free by a person's work unit, were converted into apartments and sold on the new real estate markets

60

Free Response Question

Define the term "placelessness" as used in human geography. Give examples of placelessness in the United States. Describe how placelessness spreads around the globe, and comment on the consequences of placelessness as its manifestations diffuse to non-Western societies.

CHAPTER 5: IDENTITY: RACE, ETHNICITY, GENDER, AND SEXUALITY

Chapter Summary (from page 162)

Identity is a powerful concept. The way we make sense of ourselves is a personal journey that is mediated and influenced by the political, social, and cultural contexts in which we live and work. Group identities such as gender, ethnicity, race, and sexuality are constructed, both by self-realization and by identifying against and across scales. When learning about new places and different people, humans are often tempted to put places and people into boxes, into myths or stereotypes that make them easily digestible.

The geographer, especially one who spends time in the field, recognizes that how people shape and create places varies across time and space and that time, space, and place shape people, both individually and in groups. Geographer James Curtis described well the work of a geographer who studies places: "But like popular images and stereotypical portrayals of all places—whether positive or negative, historical or contemporary—these mask a reality on the ground that is decidedly more complex and dynamic, from both the economic and social perspectives." What Curtis says about places is true about people as well. What we may *think* to be positive identities, such as the myths of "Orientalism" or of the "model minority," and what we know are negative social ills, such as racism and dowry deaths, are all decidedly more complex and dynamic than they first seem.

Key Questions

1. What is identity, and how are identities constructed?
2. How do places affect identity, and how can we see identities in places?
3. How does geography reflect and shape power relationships among groups?

Field Notes

(139-141)   Building Walls

(148)   Washington Heights, New York

(155)   Water-related disease risk

(158)   Working women of Botswana

Thinking Geographically

(149) Recall the last time you were asked to check a box for your race. Does that box factor into how you make sense of yourself individually, locally, regionally, nationally, and globally?

(153) In the 2000 Census, the government tallied the number of households where a same-sex couple (with or without children) lived. Study the map of same-sex households by census tract in Figure 5.10. What gay men and lesbian women are not being counted on this map? How would the map change if sexuality were one of the "boxes" every person filled out on the census?

(162) Geographers who study race, ethnicity, gender, or sexuality are interested in the power relationships embedded in a place from which assumptions about "others" are formed or reinforced. Consider your own place, your campus, or locality. What power relationships are embedded in this place?

Chapter Outline

A. What Is Identity, And How Are Identities Constructed?
   1. Race
   2. Racism in the United States
   3. Residential Segregation
   4. Identities across Scales
   5. The Scale of New York City
B. How Do Places Affect Identity, And How Can We See Identities in Places?
   1. Ethnicity and Place
      Chinatown in Mexicali
   2. Identity and Space
      Sexuality and Space
C. How Does Geography Reflect And Shape Power Relationships Among Groups Of People?
   1. Just Who Counts?
   2. Vulnerable Populations
   3. Women in Subsaharan Africa
   4. Dowry Deaths in India
   5. Shifting Power Relationships among Ethnic Groups
      Power Relations in Los Angeles

Chapter Figures and Tables

Figure	Page	Type	Theme
5.1	139	photo	Bedugul, Indonesia (brick-making on island of Bali)
5.2	142	photo	United States (US Census categories)
5.3	143	photo	Darwin, Australia (Aborigines)
T5.1	144	graph	Population of the United States by Race, 2000
T5.2	145	graph	Estimated Percentage of the U.S. Population by Race and Ethnicity until 2050
5.4	146	map	Residential Segregation of African Americans in Milwaukee, Wisconsin
5.5	147	map	Residential Segregation of Hispanics/Latinos and Asians. Pacific Islanders in Baltimore, Maryland
5.6	147	photo	West Palm Beach, Florida (campaigning for Bush/Cheney)
5.7	148	photo	Washington Heights, Upper Manhattan (Dominican immigrants)
5.8	150	photo	New Glarus, Wisconsin (Swiss-American town)
5.9	151	map	Chinatown in Mexicali, Mexico
5.10	152	map	Same Sex Households in New York, 2000
5.11	153	photo	Belfast, Northern Ireland (signs of conflict)
5.12	154	photo	South Korea, informal economy
5.13	155	photo	Northern Pakistan, children by ditch
5.14	156-157	map	Gender Empowerment Measure
5.15	158	photo	Kanye, Botswana, working women
5.16	159	photo	Noida, India, story of Nisha Sharma
5.17	161	map	The Changing Ethnic Composition of South-Central Los Angeles, 1960-1980

Exercise for Chapter Figures and Tables

Look at Figure 5.12, a photo of Korean women selling farm produce near an ancient temple. Consider these questions:

- Is South Korea not one of the "Little Dragons" of East Asia, a newly industrialized country (NIC); are such scenes typical in these wealthier countries?
- Notice how the women are squatting, a position they can hold for hours (as can Asian men). Can you squat comfortably, flat-footed? Give it a try. In what ways is the ability to squat in such a manner useful?
- The informal economy exists in all countries, even the most developed ones. Give examples of the informal economy in your city.
- What is the relevance of this photo to the theme of this chapter?

Geographic Concepts

Geographic Concepts (Glossary of Terms)		
gender	residential segregation	place
identity	succession	gendered
identifying against	sense of place	queer theory
race	ethnicity	dowry deaths
racism	space	barrioization

Quiz for Geographic Concepts

Match the term with the definition.

1. ____ barrioization

2. ____ residential segregation

3. ____ racism

4. ____ gender

5. ____ identity

6. ____ queer theory

7. ____ place

8. ____ ethnicity

9. ____ space

10. ____ race

11. ____ identifying against

12. ____ succession

A. Social differences between men and women, rather than anatomical, biological differences between the sexes.

B. The dramatic increase in Hispanic population in a given neighborhood.

C. How we make sense of ourselves, how people see themselves at different scales.

D. State of mind derived through the infusion of a place with meaning and emotion by remembering important events that occurred in that place.

E. In the context of arranged marriages in India, disputes over the price to be paid by the family of the bride to the father of the groom which have, in some extreme cases, led to the death of the bride.

F. Constructing an identity by first defining the "other" and then defining ourselves as "not the other."

G. Social relations stretched out.

H. Uniqueness of a location.

13. _____ dowry deaths

14. _____ gendered

15. _____ sense of place

I.   The degree to which two or more groups live separately from one another in different parts of the urban environment.

J.   Theory that highlights the contextual nature of opposition to the heteronormative and focuses on the political engagement of "queers" with the heteronormative.

K.   A categorization of humans based on skin color and other physical characteristics; social and political constructions based on ideas that some biological differences are more important than others.

L.   Process by which new immigrants to a city move to and dominate or take over areas or neighborhoods occupied by older immigrant groups.

M.   In terms of a place, whether the place is designed for or claimed by men or women.

N.   Frequently referred to as a system or attitude toward visible differences in individuals, an ideology of difference that ascribes significance and meaning to culturally, socially, and politically constructed ideas based on phenotypical features.

O.   Affiliation or identity within a group of people bound by common ancestry and culture.

Chapter Related Internet Links

Learn More Online

About the Gay and Lesbian Atlas
http://www.urban.org/pubs/gayatlas/

About Racial and Ethnic Segregation in the United States, 1980-2000
http://www.census.gov/hhes/www/housing/resseg/papertoc.html

About the Murals in Northern Ireland
http://cain.ulst.ac.uk/mccormick/intro.html

Watch It Online

About Ethnicity and the City
http://www.learner.org/resources/series180.html#program_descriptions
click on Video On Demand for "Boston Ethnic Mosaic"
About Ethnic Fragmentation in Canada
http://www.learner.org/resources/series180.html#program_descriptions
click on Video On Demand for "Vancouver: Hong Kong East" and "Montreal: An Island of French"

About Migration and Identity
http://www.learner.org/resources/series85.html#program_descriptions
click on Video On Demand for "A Migrant's Heart"

Exercise for Chapter Related Internet Links

Watch the video program "Vancouver: Hong Kong East" (about 12 minutes). Additionally, read the Wikipedia article on Hong Kong (http://en.wikipedia.org/wiki/Hong_Kong). Discuss the following questions:

- Is your city as multicultural as Vancouver? What are the largest ethnic minorities and recent immigrant populations in your location?
- Do you feel a city improves by immigrant waves? If yes, in what ways?
- The tear-down, rebuild with McMansions phenomenon is common in many North American cities. Is this a good thing or bad thing? Why?
- What factors prompted the wave of Hong Kong relocation and investment to Vancouver? Why did the trend reverse?
- Do you think immigrant populations have an obligation to assimilate into their new society?

Compare what you learned in this video to the Los Angeles suburb of Monterey Park and the neighboring towns in the San Gabriel Valley (see: http://en.wikipedia.org/wiki/Little_Taipei).

APHG-Type Questions

Note: Be sure to take the online Self Tests on the Student Companion Site.
Check answer key at the end of the workbook.

Multiple Choice Questions

Type A: Basic Knowledge.

1. How does "ethnicity" differ from "race?"
   A. there is no difference in common usage
   B. ethnicity implies a religious affiliation, race does not
   C. race is a physiological concept, ethnicity is not linked to genetics
   D. race is something to which we choose to belong; ethnicity is assigned
   E. ethnicity is something to which we choose to belong; race is assigned

2. According to a 2002 US Census Bureau report
   A. overall residential segregation by race/ethnicity was on the decline
   B. overall residential segregation by race/ethnicity was on the increase
   C. reported acts of racial discrimination were down between 1990 and 2000
   D. Korean immigrants are the most cohesive ethnic group in the U.S.
   E. Chinese are the most assimilated minority in the U.S.

3. Which regional population group is combined with Asian in the US Census Bureau classification?
   A. Siberians
   B. Pacific Islanders
   C. Mongolians
   D. South Asians
   E. East Indians

4. What U.S. city has the greatest number and diversity of immigrants?
   A. Chicago
   B. Los Angeles
   C. Miami
   D. New York
   E. Seattle

5. State of mind derived through the infusion of a place with meaning and emotion.
   A. sense of place
   B. ethnicity
   C. ethnic space
   D. queer theory
   E. barrioization

6. Who produces about 70% of the food in rural Sub-Saharan Africa?
   A. men
   B. women
   C. children
   D. agribusiness companies
   E. immigrants

7. For what is Nisha Sharma famous?
   A. she appeared on Oprah in 2004
   B. she started a shelter for battered women in India
   C. she was the first female in her village to get a college education
   D. she was murdered by her husband because her family gave an insufficient dowry
   E. she called off her wedding when the groom's family demanded a higher dowry

8. Barrioization refers to
   A. the increasing political clout of Mexican immigrants in big city politics
   B. the replacement of Anglo-American street names with Spanish street names
   C. neighborhoods, especially in Los Angeles, where the Hispanic population rapidly displaces the original residents
   D. the gerrymandering of voting districts in predominantly Hispanic regions
   E. states where Hispanics will represent a majority population in the next 20 years

9. The most residentially segregated large metropolitan area for African Americans.
   A. Detroit, MI
   B. Orange County, CA
   C. San Francisco, CA
   D. Milwaukee, WI
   E. New York, NY

10. In New York, Puerto Ricans took over Jewish neighborhoods in a process geographers call
    A. residential segregation
    B. ethnic succession
    C. residential invasion
    D. cultural transition
    E. invasion and succession

Type B: Application

1. Which of the following demographic trends occurred in Los Angeles between the 1990 and 2000 censuses?
    A. Korean immigrants were the fastest growing ethnic group
    B. the Hispanic population grew from 39% to 46%
    C. the black population declined in total and relative numbers
    D. Korean businesses moved northward out of South-Central LA
    E. as Hispanic immigrants prospered, they relocated to the Valley

2. What would happen to the world's Gross National Income if the work women do at home was calculated at market value?
    A. there is no way to accurately estimate the value of such work
    B. global GNI would remain the same
    C. global GNI would actually decline
    D. global GNI would grow by 10%
    E. global GNI would grow by about 1/3rd

3. Which of the following best describes relations between Indians and Pakistanis in Fairfax County, Virginia?
    A. they maintain separate food and entertainment businesses
    B. they are spatially segregated in different neighborhoods
    C. they attend the same Hindu temples
    D. they coexist without animosity
    E. tensions occasionally require police intervention

4. In the United States, racial categories are imposed on people by all of the following EXCEPT
    A. residential segregation
    B. mandatory school segregation
    C. racialized divisions of labor
    D. race categories in the U.S. Census
    E. race-oriented movies and comic strips

5. A term used in the discussion of sexual behavior, gender, and society, primarily within the fields of queer theory and gender theory. It is used to describe (and frequently to criticize) the manner in which many social institutions and social policies are seen to reinforce certain beliefs.
    A. transgender
    B. sexual identity
    C. gendered roles
    D. identity
    E. heteronormative

Free Response Question

Compare the two maps of a community college district. The areal units represent Census Places (incorporated towns and villages in the Chicago west suburbs).

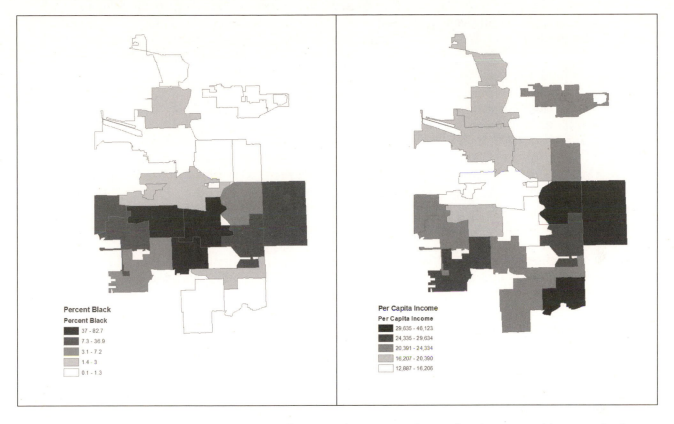

In what ways do the spatial patterns confirm or reject our notions about race and income in the United States?

CHAPTER 6: LANGUAGE

Chapter Summary (from page 192)

The global mosaic of languages reflects centuries of divergence, convergence, extinction, and diffusion. Linguists and linguistic geographers have the interesting work of uncovering, through deep reconstruction, the hearths of the world's language families. Some languages, such as Basque, defy explanation. Other languages are the foci of countless studies, many of which come to differing conclusions about their ancient origins.

As certain languages, such as English and Chinese, gain speakers and become global languages, other languages become extinct. Some languages persist by becoming the lingua franca of a region or place. Governments choose official languages, and through public schools, educators entrench an official language in a place. Many countries, faced with the global diffusion of the English language, defend and promote their national language. Whether requiring signs to be written a certain way or requiring a television station to broadcast some proportion of programming in the national language, governments can preserve language, choose a certain dialect as the standard, or repel the diffusion of other languages.

Regardless of the place, the people, or the language used, language continues to define, shape, and maintain culture. How a person thinks about the world is reflected in the words used to describe and define it.

Key Questions

1. What are languages, and what role do languages play in culture?
2. Why are languages distributed the way they are?
3. How do languages diffuse?
4. What role does language play in making places?

Field Notes

(164-168)   What Should I say? What language to use in Brussels, Belgium.

(191)   Greenville, North Carolina, Martin Luther King, Jr. Drive

Thinking Geographically

(174) Linguist Bert Vaux's study of dialects in American English points to the differences in words for common things such as soft drinks and sandwiches. Describe a time when you said something and a speaker of another dialect did not understand the word you used. Where did the person with whom you were speaking come from? Was the word a term for a common thing? Why do you think dialects have different words for common things, things found across dialects, such as soft drinks and sandwiches?

(184) Education also affects the distribution of languages across the globe and within regions and countries. Thinking about different regions of the world, consider how education plays a role in the distribution of English speakers. Who learns English in each of these regions and why? What role does education play in the global distribution of English speakers?

(187) Choose a country in the world. Imagine you become a strong leader of a centralized government in the country. Pick a language used in the country other than the tongue spoken by the majority. Determine what policies you could put in place to make the minority language an official language of the country. What reactions would your initiative generate? Who would support it and who would not?

(191) *This place was first named by Gabrielino Indians. In 1769, Spanish Franciscan priests renamed the place. In 1850, English speakers renamed the place.* Do not use the Internet to help you. Use only maps in this book or in atlases to help you deduce what this place is. Maps of European exploration and colonialism will help you the most. Look at the end of the chapter summary for the answer.

Chapter Outline

A. What Are Languages, And What Role Do Languages Play In Cultures?
  1. Language and Culture
  2. What is Language?
  3. Standardized Language
  4. Dialects
B. Why Are Languages Distributed The Way They Are?
  1. Language Formation
    a. Reconstructing the Vocabulary of Proto-Indo-European and Its Ancient Ancestor
    b. Locating the Hearth of Proto-Indo-European
    c. Tracing the Routes of Diffusion of Proto-Indo-European
  2. The Languages of Europe
  3. Languages of Subsaharan Africa
C. How Do Languages Diffuse?
  1. Lingua Franca
  2. Multilingualism
  3. Official Languages
  4. Global Language
D. What Role Does Language Play In Making Places?
  Changing Toponyms
    a. Post-Colonial Toponyms
    b. Postrevolution Toponyms
    c. Memorial Toponyms
    d. Commodification of Toponyms

Chapter Figures and Tables

Figure	Page	Type	Theme
6.1	164	photo	Brussels, Belgium (bi-lingual McDonald's)
6.2	166	map	Languages of Europe
6.3	167	map	Divided Belgium
6.4	169	graph	Languages Used on the Internet
6.5	170	map	Percent of People 5 Years and Older Who Speak a Language other than English at Home in the United States
T6.1	171	table	Top Ten Languages Spoken at Home by Non-English Speakers in the United States
6.6	171	photo	Quebec Province, Quebec (French Canadian culture)
6.7	173	map	Common Name for a Soft Drink in the United States, by State, 2002
6.8	174-175	map	Language Families of the World
6.9	178	illustration	Indo-European Branches of the Language Tree

6.10	179	map	The Renfrew Hypothesis
6.11	180	map	Indo-European Language Family: Proposed Westward Dispersal
6.12	180	map	Indo-European Language Family: Proposed Hearth and Dispersal Hypothesis
6.13	182	photo	San Sebastian, Spain (graffiti)
6.14	182	map	Language Families of Africa
6.15	183	map	Nigeria: Generalized Ethnolinguistic Areas
6.16	185	photo	Dubai, United Arab Emirates (lingua franca)
6.17	186	map	Language Families of India
6.18	189	photo	Llanfairpwllgwyngyllgogerychwyrndrobwllllantysiliogogogoch, Wales
6.19	190	map	Cities in the United States with a Street Named for Martin Luther King, Jr.
6.20	191	photo	Greenville, North Carolina (Martin Luther King, Jr. Drive)

Exercises for Chapter Figures and Tables

Look at Figure 6.9, Indo-European Branches of the Language Tree. Discuss these questions:

- What languages are most closely related to English?
- The whole tree would be at a macro (global) linguistic scale. The Indo-European part of the tree might be considered mesoscale, and the English branch microscale. If we took the scale down even further (made the scale larger) such that twigs were branching off the English branch, what would those twigs represent?
- Discuss the language tree in terms of language evolution, and language evolution in terms of human migrations.
- Read the poem below. Can you tell what language it is? Does it sound like any modern language with which you are familiar? (For the answer, ask an English teacher)

> Whan that aprill with his shoures soote
> The droghte of march hath perced to the roote,
> And bathed every veyne in swich licour
> Of which vertu engendred is the flour;
> Whan zephirus eek with his sweete breeth
> Inspired hath in every holt and heeth
> Tendre croppes, and the yonge sonne
> Hath in the ram his halve cours yronne,
> And smale foweles maken melodye,
> That slepen al the nyght with open ye
> (so priketh hem nature in hir corages);
> Thanne longen folk to goon on pilgrimages,

Geographic Concepts

Geographic Concepts (Glossary of Terms)		
language	backward reconstruction	Slavic languages
culture	extinct language	lingua franca
standard language	deep reconstruction	pidgin language
dialects	nostratic	Creole language
isogloss	language divergence	monolingual states
mutual intelligibility	language convergence	multilingual states
dialect chains	Renfrew hypothesis	official language
language families	conquest theory	global language

subfamilies	dispersal hypothesis	place
sound shift	Romance languages	toponym
Proto-Indo-European	Germanic languages	

Quiz for Geographic Concepts

Match the term with the definition.

1. _____ lingua franca

2. _____ nostratic

3. _____ dialects

4. _____ toponym

5. _____ sound shift

6. _____ language convergence

7. _____ official language

8. _____ Renfrew hypothesis

9. _____ Creole language

10. _____ language families

11. _____ backward reconstruction

12. _____ dispersal hypothesis

13. _____ mutual intelligibility

14. _____ isogloss

15. _____ monolingual states

A. Countries in which more than one language is spoken.

B. A geographic boundary within which a particular linguistic feature occurs.

C. The ability of two people to understand each other when speaking.

D. A language that began as a pidgin language but was later adopted as the mother tongue by a people in place of the mother tongue.

E. Group of languages with a shared by fairly distant origin.

F. Place name.

G. Slight change in a word across languages within a subfamily or through a language family from the present backward towards its origin.

H. The collapsing of two languages into one resulting from the consistent spatial interaction of peoples with different languages.

I. The tracking of sound shifts and hardening of consonants backward toward the original language.

J. A common language used among speakers of different languages for the purpose of trade and commerce.

K. Proposition that holds that the Indo-European languages that arose from Proto-Indo-European were first carried eastward into Southwest Asia, next around the Caspian Sea, and then across the Russian-Ukrainian plains and on into the Balkans.

L. Proposal that three areas in and near the first agricultural hearth, the Fertile Crescent, gave rise to three language families: Europe's Indo-European languages; North Africa and Arabian languages; the languages in present-day Iran, Afghanistan, Pakistan and India.

M. Local or regional characteristics of a language. In addition to pronunciation variation, has distinctive vocabulary and grammar.

N. Language believed to be the ancestral language not only of Proto-Indo-European, but also of the Kartvelian languages of the southern Caucasus region, the Uralic-Altaic languages, the Dravidian languages, and the Afro-Asiatic language family.

O. In multilingual countries the language selected, often by the educated and politically powerful elite, to promote internal cohesion.

Chapter Related Internet Links

Learn More Online

About Bert Vaux's Survey of American Dialects
http://www.cfprod01.imt.uwm.edu/Dept/FLL/linguistics/dialect/index.html

About Learning Foreign Languages On-Line
http://www.bbc.co.uk/languages/

Watch It Online

About the Loss of Native Languages in Alaska
http://www.learner.org/resources/series85.html#program_descriptions
click on Video On Demand for "Alaska: The Last Frontier?"

About Stephen Oppenheimer's Theory
http://www.nhm.ac.uk/darwincentre/live/presentations/presentation_290703StephenOppenheimer.html

Exercises for Chapter Related Internet Links

The link to the Stephen Oppenheimer's Theory video no longer works, so read about his theory at:

   http://www.accampbell.uklinux.net/bookreviews/r/oppenheimer.html

As you read about the out-of-Africa theory, look at the following human migrations maps based on DNA evidence:

   http://www.mitosearch.org/migration_map_new.pdf

Discuss the following questions:

• Is there any controversy between the DNA evidence and archeological evidence of human evolution and migration?

- If the evidence proves to be true, that all humans today are descended from a small group of homo sapiens that relatively recently (~85,000 years ago) migrated out of Africa, what are the implications for such concepts (in Chapter Five) as identity, race, racism, and ethnicity?
- How does this evidence relate to the Biblical account of creation? Does this evidence complicate the creation (or intelligent design) vs. evolution debate?
- Consider the movements of humans illustrated in the map in light of the spatial-temporal changes to Earth's physical landscape during the advance and retreat of glaciers in the late Pleistocene, and how it impacted human settlement of the planet.

APHG-Type Questions

Note: Be sure to take the online Self Tests on the Student Companion Site.
Check answer key at the end of the workbook.

Multiple Choice Questions

Type A: Basic Knowledge Questions

1. The predominant languages spoken on Madagascar are not of an African language family but belong to
   A. Indo-European family
   B. Sino-Tibetan family
   C. Dravidian family
   D. Austronesian family
   E. Altaic family

2. Two Russian scholars have established the core of what they believe is a pre-Proto-Indo-European language named
   A. Nostratic
   B. Anatolian
   C. Etruscan
   D. Austronesian
   E. Aryano-Armenic

3. A geographic boundary within which a particular linguistic feature occurs is called a/an
   A. isotherm
   B. sound shift
   C. international border
   D. cultural boundary
   E. isolgloss

4. Hawaii and Louisiana are examples with
   A. no linguistic variation
   B. official "English only" policies
   C. official bilingual policies
   D. no official language policies
   E. Creole populations

5. Which of the following European countries has a rather sharp division between Flemish speakers in the north and Walloon speakers in the south?
   A. the Netherlands
   B. Belgium
   C. Denmark
   D. Andorra
   E. Switzerland

6. The Indo-European language family prevails on the map of Europe. Which country listed below has a language which is not in the Indo-European family?
   A. France
   B. Italy
   C. Iceland
   D. Luxembourg
   E. Hungary

7. Bantu migrations marginalized this once widespread African language family which now is found only in dry regions of southwestern Africa.
   A. Niger-Congo family
   B. Khoisan family
   C. Afro-Asiatic family
   D. Sudanic subfamily
   E. Gaelic subfamily

8. The linguistic map of Nigeria reflects extreme fragmentation with nearly _____ languages spoken.
   A. 15
   B. 25
   C. 200
   D. 400
   E. 600

9. In an attempt to deal with linguistic as well as cultural diversity, many former African colonies have taken as their official language
   A. the most widely-spoken indigenous language
   B. an Austronesian and therefore neutral language
   C. the language of the former colonial power
   D. an invented language with no historical connections
   E. Swahili, the lingua franca

10. When African colonies became independent countries, one of the first acts of many of the new governments was to
    A. conduct a census
    B. build a new capital city
    C. change the names of places that had been named after colonial figures
    D. build new road systems
    E. seek international aid

Type B: Application Questions

1. The French government has _____ to protect French language and culture.
   A. banned foreign words in advertising and on radio and television
   B. established the Académie Française to standardize the language
   C. passed a law levying fines on those using foreign terms
   D. amended the constitution to make French the official language
   E. all of the above

2. In technically advanced societies there is likely to be
   A. a standard language
   B. many basic languages
   C. limited expansion of language
   D. standard pronunciation
   E. a lot of technical terms

3. Dialects are most often marked by actual differences in
   A. accents
   B. pronunciation
   C. vocabulary
   D. syntax
   E. diction

4. Convergence processes yielding a synthesis of several languages produce a pidgin language. When this language becomes the first language of a population it is referred to as a
   A. dialect
   B. creole language
   C. language subfamily
   D. lingua franca
   E. corrupted language

5. Official languages such as Spanish and Quechuan in Peru or English and Pilipino in the Philippines reflect
   A. linguist divergence
   B. the country's history
   C. creolization
   D. linguas franca
   E. confusion about language identity

Free Response Question

Consider the blank map of India.

1. What are the three largest language families represented by the twenty-two official languages of India?

2. Identify the language family that predominates in the regions covered by numbers 1 through 3, and give an example of one specific language within that region.

3. Explain why India is such an important region for the outsourcing of American services despite its linguistic complexity.

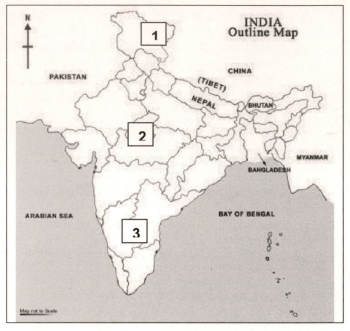

CHAPTER 7: RELIGION

Chapter Summary (from page 217)

Religion is a major force in shaping and changing culture. The major world religions today all stem from an area of Eurasia stretching from the Eastern Mediterranean to China. Major world religions are distributed regionally, with Hinduism in India; Buddhism, Taoism, Shintoism, and Chinese philosophies in East and Southeast Asia; Islam reaching across North Africa, through the Middle East and into Southeast Asia; Shamanist religions mainly in Subsaharan Africa; and Christianity in Europe, Western Asia, the Americas, Australia and New Zealand. Judaism, another major world religion, is not as concentrated. Today Judaism has a base in Israel and has adherents scattered throughout Europe and the Americas.

As the September 11, 2001 attacks on New York City and Washington, D.C. made clear, religious beliefs can drive people to extremist behaviors. On a day-to-day basis, however, religion more typically drives cultures—shaping how people behave, how people perceive the behaviors of others, and how people across place, scale, and time interact with each other.

Key Questions

1. What is religion and what role does it play in culture?
2. Where did the world's major religions originate, and how do religions diffuse?
3. How is religion seen in the cultural landscape?
4. What role does religion play in ethnic conflict?

Field Notes

(196)   Dying and Resurrecting. The former Soviet Union.

(205)   Prague, Czech Republic. The Old Jewish Cemetery.

(213)   Ardmore, Ireland. St. Declan's Holy Well.

(216)   India Bonalu Festival. Golconda Fort, Hyderabad.

(217)   Yangon, Myanmar. The golden Shwedogon Pagoda in the heart of Yangon.

Thinking Geographically

(197)   Describe how religion and language affect and change each other to shape cultures. (Consider what happens to a society's religion and language when a different religion or language diffuses to the place.)

(212) Migration plays a large role in the diffusion of religions, both universalizing and ethnic. As Europe becomes more secular, migrants from outside of Europe continue to settle in the region. Imagine Europe 30 years from now. Predict where in Europe secularism will be the most prominent and where religious adherence will strengthen.

(223) Choose a pilgrimage site, such as Mecca, Vatican City, or the Western Wall, and describe how the act of pilgrimage (in some cases by millions) alters this place's cultural landscape and environment.

(235) Boal's studies in Northern Ireland demonstrate that solving a religious conflict is typically not about theology; it is about identity. You are assigned the potentially Nobel Prize–winning task of "solving" the conflict either in Northern Ireland or in Israel and Palestine. Using Boal's example, determine how you can alter activity spaces and change identities to create the conditions for long-lasting peace in one of these major conflict zones.

Chapter Outline

A. What Is Religion and What Role Does it Play in Culture?
B. Where Did the World's Major Religions Originate, and How Do Religions Diffuse?
    1. The World Map of Religions Today
    2. From the Hearth of South Asia
        a. Hinduism
        b. Diffusion of Hinduism
        c. Buddhism
        d. Shintoism
    3. From the Hearth of the Huang He River Valley
        a. Taoism
        b. Confucianism
        c. Diffusion of Chinese Religions
    4. From the Hearth of the Eastern Mediterranean
        a. Judaism
        b. Diffusion of Judaism
        c. Christianity
        d. Diffusion of Christianity
        e. Islam
        f. Diffusion of Islam
        g. Traditional and Shamanist
        h. The Rise of Secularism
C. How is Religion Seen in the Cultural Landscape?
    1. Sacred Sites of Jerusalem
    2. Landscapes of Hinduism and Buddhism
    3. Landscapes of Christianity
        a. Religious Landscapes in the United States
    4. Landscapes of Islam
D. What Role Does Religion Play in Ethnic Conflict?
    1. Conflicts along Religious Borders
    2. Israel and Palestine
    3. The Horn of Africa
    4. The Former Yugoslavia
    5. Northern Ireland
    6. Religious Fundamentalism and Extremism
        a. Christianity
        b. Judaism
        c. Islam

Chapter Figures and Tables

Figure	Page	Type	Theme
7.1	193	photo	Vyshniyvolochek, Russia (Russian Orthodox church)
7.2	194	map	Nagorno-Karabakh and Nakhichevan
7.3	196	photo	Mombasa, Kenya (Hindi crematorium)
7.4	196	photo	Antwerp, Belgium (cathedral)
7.5	197	chart	Hearths of Major World Religions
7.6	198-199	map	Religions of the World
T7.1	200	table	Adherent to Major World Religions
7.7	200	photo	Angkor Wat, Cambodia (temple complex)
7.8	201	map	Diffusion of Four Major World Religions
7.9	202	photo	Borobudur, Indonesia (Buddhist complex)
7.10	203	photo	Kyoto, Japan (Shinto shrine)
7.11	205	photo	Prague, Czech Republic (Jewish cemetery)
7.12	207	map	The Roman Empire, Divided into East and West
7.13	207	map	Religions in Switzerland
7.14	208	photo	La Chinantla, Mexico (Catholic missionaries)
7.15	209	photo	Kota Kinabalu, Malaysia (Sabah State Mosque)
7.16	210	map	Diffusion of Islam
7.17	211	photo	Paris, France (Islamic mosques)
7.18	211	map	Indigenous Religions
7.19	213	photo	Ardmore, Ireland (Catholic pilgrimage site)
7.20	214	photo	Jerusalem, Israel (Western Wall and Dome of the Rock Mosque)
7.21	215	photo	Jerusalem, Israel (Church of the Holy Sepulcher)
7.22	216	photo	Varanasi, India (ritual bathing in the Ganges)
7.23	216	photo	India Bonalu Festival
7.24	217	photo	Yangon, Myanmar (Buddhist pagoda/stupa)
7.25	218	photo	Bordeaux, France (Saint Michael's Tower)
7.26	218	photo	Singapore (Saint Andrew's Cathedral)
7.27	219	photo	Vatican City (Pope John Paul II)
7.28	220	map	Major Religious Regions of the United States
7.29	221	map	Bosnia and Herzegovina
7.30	221	photo	Brown County, South Dakota (Scandinavian Lutheran Church)
7.31	221	photo	Zell, South Dakota (St. Mary's Catholic Church)
7.32	222	photo	Isfahan, Iran (mosque, Islamic architecture)
7.33	223	photo	Mecca, Saudi Arabia (Grand Mosque and Kaaba)
7.34	224	map	African Transition Zone
7.35	226	photo	Kfar Darom, Gaza Strip (Israeli army withdrawal from Gaza Strip)
7.36	227	map	The West Bank
7.37	228	map	Religious Regions in the Horn of Africa
7.38	230	map	The Former Yugoslavia (pre-war distribution of ethnic groups)
7.39	231	map	Bosnia and Herzegovina (distribution of ethnic groups)
7.40	232	map	Religious Affiliation in Northern Ireland
7.41	235	photo	New York, New York (World Trade Center on 9/11)

Exercise for Chapter Figures and Tables

Review Figure 7.38, The Former Yugoslavia.

- What might be a better name for this map?
- Photocopy the map, then label each of the colored regions with a capital letter. Determine what religion is represented by each letter.
- What are the historical processes that led to this religious diversity?

- Read more about the written scripts at: http://www.omniglot.com/writing/serbo-croat.htm.
- Discuss this region in terms of three variables of ethnicity:
  - religion
  - spoken language
  - written language (script)

Geographic Concepts

Geographic Concepts (Glossary of Terms)		
religion	Confucianism	pilgrimage
secularism	Judaism	sacred site
monotheistic religion	diaspora	minarets
polytheistic religion	Zionism	hajj
animistic religion	Christianity	interfaith boundaries
universalizing religion	Eastern Orthodox Church	intrafaith boundaries
ethnic religion	Roman Catholic Church	genocide
Hinduism	Protestant	activity space
caste system	Islam	religious fundamentalism
Buddhism	Sunni	religious extremism
Shintoism	Shi'ite	shari'a law
Taoism	Shamanism	jihad
Feng Shui		

Quiz for Geographic Concepts

Match the term with a definition.

1. _____ Islam

2. _____ religious extremism

3. _____ secularism

4. _____ Taoism

5. _____ genocide

6. _____ hajj

7. _____ Eastern Orthodox

8. _____ intrafaith boundaries

9. _____ universalizing religion

10. _____ caste system

11. _____ Zionism

12. _____ Confucianism

A. The youngest of the major world religions, based on the teachings of Muhammad.

B. The idea that ethical and moral standards should be formulated and adhered to for life on Earth, not to accommodate the prescriptions of a deity and promises of a comfortable afterlife.

C. The systematic killing or extermination of an entire people or nation.

D. A religion that is particular to one, culturally distinct, group of people.

E. Voluntary travel by an adherent to a sacred site to pay respects or participate in a ritual at the site.

F. The movement to unite the Jewish people of the diaspora and to establish a national homeland for them in the promised land.

G. Boundaries within a single major faith.

13. ____ pilgrimage

14. ____ diaspora

15. ____ ethnic religion

H. One of the three major branches of Christianity; arose out of the division of the Roman Empire into four governmental regions; centered in Constantinople (Istanbul).

I. A philosophy of ethics, education, and public service based on the writings of Confucius and traditionally thought of as one of the core elements of Chinese culture

J. The strict social segregation of people on the basis of ancestry and occupation.

K. Religious fundamentalism carried to the point of violence.

L. Religion believed to have been founded by Lao-Tsu (Laozi) and based upon his book entitled *Book of the Way*.

M. The Muslim pilgrimage to Mecca, the birthplace of Muhammad.

N. A belief system that espouses the idea that there is one true religion that is universal in scope; adherents often believe their religion represents universal truths that are spread through evangelism and missionary work.

O. A term describing forceful or voluntary dispersal of a people from their homeland to a new place. Originally applied to the Jews, but now used for other population dispersals.

Chapter Related Internet Links

Learn More Online

About Devil's Tower
http://www.nps.gov/deto/place.htm

About Religions of the World
http://www.bbc.co.uk/worldservice/people/features/world_religions/index.shtml

About the Sacred Sites in Jerusalem
http://news.bbc.co.uk/hi/english/static/in_depth/middle_east/2000/holy_places/default.stm

Watch It Online

Christianity in European History
http://www.learner.org/resources/series58.html#program_descriptions
click Video On Demand

The Confucian Tradition
http://www.learner.org/resources/series144.html#program_descriptions
click Video On Demand

Exercises for Chapter Related Internet Links

It is well known that Israel/Palestine is the hearth of two of the world's great religions, Judaism and Christianity, and hosts the third most sacred place for a third—Islam. All three faiths contest many of the sites sacred to one or all of the three religions, most of which are in the Jerusalem/West Bank region. Some geographers specialize in the geography of shared sacred space.

Israel also hosts a fourth global religion, the Bahá'í Faith, spatially the second largest religion in the world, whose World Centre is located on the north slope of Mount Carmel in Haifa, and whose most sacred place is across the Bay of Haifa near the predominantly Palestinian town of Akka. The Bahá'í Faith properties are not contested by other religions and thus do not prevent Bahá'í pilgrims from visiting these sites.

Visit the two web sites above:
- Sacred Sites in Jerusalem
- Other Sacred Sites in Israel

Discuss the phenomenon of how one small geographic region came to be such an important focal point of religion, and a flash point for conflict in modern times.

Consider also in what ways these four religions differ from other spatially significant faiths such Hinduism, Buddhism and the religions of East Asia.

APHG-Type Questions

Note: Be sure to take the online Self Tests on the Student Companion Site.
Check answer key at the end of the workbook.

Multiple Choice Questions

Type A: Basic Knowledge.

1. The vote to partition Palestine was taken by
   A. Israel
   B. the United Nations
   C. Britain
   D. the Ottoman Empire
   E. League of Nations

2. Which of the following Balkan association is **incorrect**?
    A. Slovenian—Catholic
    B. Croat—Orthodox
    C. Serbian—Cyrillic alphabet
    D. Montenegrans—Orthodox
    E. Bosnian—Muslim

3. The ideology of Zionism has as its goal
    A. the merger of Judaism with other religions
    B. the merger of the three modern divisions of Judaism
    C. a homeland for the Jewish people
    D. the elimination of the Orthodox division within the faith
    E. the search for the true Mount Zion where the Ten Commandments were revealed

4. The youngest major religion is
    A. Hinduism
    B. Judaism
    C. Islam
    D. Christianity
    E. Bahá'í Faith

5. Modern-day Shiah Islam dominates a region centered on
    A. Pakistan
    B. Arabia
    C. Armenia
    D. Indonesia
    E. Iran

6. The Hajj, one of the "pillars of Islam," is
    A. charitable giving
    B. fasting during the holy month
    C. the veil worn by Muslim women
    D. the pilgrimage to Mecca
    E. the five daily prayers

7. The world's largest dominantly Islamic state is
    A. Iran
    B. Pakistan
    C. Egypt
    D. Indonesia
    E. India

8. The Jews of Central Europe are known as
    A. Ashkenazim
    B. Sephardim
    C. Zionists
    D. Orthodox
    E. Reformed

9. The faith that is most widely dispersed over the world is
    A. Christianity
    B. Islam
    C. shamanism
    D. Buddhism
    E. Bahá'í Faith

10. Sikhism is a small compromise religion that arose from the confrontation between Hinduism
    and
    A. Buddhism
    B. Jainism
    C. Christianity
    D. British colonial officials
    E. Islam

Type B: Application Questions

1. Persuasion will not lead people to change the language they speak, but it can induce them
   to
    A. profess adherence to a new faith
    B. abandon their culture
    C. abandon their economic activities
    D. move to a new region
    E. watch Fear Factor

2. Zoroastrianism is similar to Islam and Christianity in that it is
    A. a world religion
    B. monotheistic
    C. a missionary religion
    D. polytheistic
    E. a desert faith in origin

3. Hinduism has not spread by expansion diffusion in modern times, but at one time it did
   spread by relocation diffusion as a result of
    A. the transportation of Indian workers abroad during the colonial period
    B. conquest by military groups
    C. forced relocation by Islamic invaders
    D. missionary activities overseas
    E. the Beatles visit to India in 1966

4. The *diaspora* of the Jews resulted from
    A. Moses' decision to leave Egypt
    B. the Arab-Israeli conflict
    C. the European holocaust of the Nazis
    D. the Roman destruction of Jerusalem
    E. disagreements between the Sadducees and the Pharisees

5. Which is NOT a feature of Islamic sacred architecture?
   A. minarets
   B. adoption of Roman models of design
   C. influenced by the architecture of other civilizations
   D. geometric and calligraphic ornamentation
   E. frescoes depicting the life of the prophet

Free Response Question

Secularism began to arise with the separation of church and state in Europe.
   - Why was this so?
   - What effect has this had on the role of tradition and the choice of personal lifestyles?
   - In what way could it be argued that Islamic fundamentalism is a reaction against liberal secularism?
   - What geographic concepts can be used to understand the tension between an Islamic East and a secular West?

CHAPTER 8: POLITCAL GEOGRAPHY

Chapter Summary (from page 272)

We tend to take the state for granted. Although the modern state idea is less than 400 years old, the idea and ideal of the nation-state have diffused around the globe, primarily through colonialism and international organizations.

The state may seem natural and permanent, but it is not. New states are being recognized, and existing states are vulnerable to many destructive forces. From organizing governments to defining and defending boundaries, to nation-building, to terrorism, to sharing or splitting sovereignty with supranational organizations, political geographers wonder what the future of the state is. How long can this way of politically organizing space last?

As we look to political organization beyond the state, we can turn to the global scale and consider what places the global world economy most affects, shapes, and benefits. In the next chapter, we study global cities—places where major links in the world economy connect and places that in many ways transcend the state.

Key Questions

1. How is space politically organized into states and nations?
2. How do states spatially organize their governments?
3. How are boundaries established, and why do boundary disputes occur?
4. How do geopolitics and critical geopolitics help us understand the world?
5. What are supranational organizations, and what is the future of the state?

Field Notes

(237)   Independence is better than servitude. Ghana.

(245)   Cluj-Napoca, Romania. Tension between ethnic Hungarians and Romanians.

(257)   Honolulu, Hawaii. Devolutionary stress on American soil.

Thinking Geographically

(252) Imagine you are the leader of a newly independent state in Africa or Asia. Determine what your government can do to build a nation that corresponds with the borders of your state. Consider the roles of education, government, military, and culture in your exercise in nation-building.

(259) Choose an example of a devolutionary movement and determine whether autonomy (self-governance) for that region would benefit the autonomous region, the country in which it is located, or both.

(262) People used to think physical-political boundaries were more stable than geometric boundaries. Through studies of many places, political geographers have confirmed that this idea is false. Construct your own argument explaining why physical-political boundaries can create just as much instability as geometric boundaries.

(265) Read a major newspaper (in print or online) and look for a recent statement by a world political leader regarding international politics. Using the concept of critical geopolitics, determine what geopolitical view of the world the leader has—how does he or she define the world spatially?

(272) In 2004, the European Union welcomed ten additional states, and in 2007, it welcomed two more. Examine the European Union website (listed below in the Learn More Online section). Read about the European Union's expansion and what is going on in the European Union right now. Assess how complicated it is for the European Union to bring together these many divergent members into one supranational organization.

Chapter Outline

A. How Is Space Politically Organized Into States And Nations?
   1. The Modern State Idea
   2. Nations
   3. Nation-State
   4. Multistate Nations, Multinational States, and Stateless Nations
   5. European Colonialism and the Diffusion of the Nation-State Model
   6. Construction of the Capitalist World Economy
   7. World-Systems and Political Power
   8. The Enduring Impact of the Nation-State Idea
B. How Do States Spatially Organize Their Governments?
   1. Form of Government
   2. Devolution
       a. Ethnocultural Devolutionary Movements
       b. Economic Devolutionary Forces
       c. Spatial Devolutionary Forces
   3. Electoral Geography
C. How Are Boundaries Established, And Why Do Boundary Disputes Occur?
   1. Establishing Boundaries
   2. Types of Boundaries
   3. Boundary Disputes
D. How Do Geopolitics And Critical Geopolitics Help Us Understand The World?
   1. Classical Geopolitics
   2. The German School
   3. The British/American School
   4. Influence of Geopoliticians on Politics
   5. Critical Geopolitics
   6. Geopolitical World Order
E. What Are Supranational Organizations, And What Is The Future Of The State?
   1. From League of Nations to United Nations
   2. Regional Supranational Organizations
   3. The European Union
   4. How Does Supranationalism Affect the State?

Chapter Figures and Tables

Figure	Page	Type	Theme
8.1	237	photo	Accra, Ghana (statue of Kwame Nkrumah)
8.2	238-239	map	Dates of Independence for States Throughout the World
8.3	242-243	map	States of the World, 2006
8.4	244	map	European Political Fragmentation in 1648
8.5	245	photo	Cluj-Napoca, Romania (St. Michael's Cathedral)
8.6	246	map	Kurdish Region of the Middle East
8.7	247	chart	Two Waves of Colonialism between 1500 and 1975
8.8	248-249	map	Dominant Colonial Influences from 1550-1950
8.9	250	painting	"Sunday on La Grande Jatte," Art Institute of Chicago.
8.10	251	map	The World Economy
8.11	253	map	Countries in Africa with Shari'a Laws
8.12	254	photo	St. Paul, Minnesota (Minnesota Children's Museum sign)
8.13	254	map	Ethnic Mosaic of Eastern Europe
8.14	255	map	Europe: Foci of Devolutionary Pressures, 2009
8.15	256	photo	Catalonia, Spain (Barcelona street scene)
8.16	257	photo	Honolulu, Hawaii (Hawaiian state flag upside down)
8.17	259	map	Electoral Geography: Florida's Third Congressional District
8.18	260	illustration	The Vertical Plane of a Political Boundary
8.19	260	map	The International Boundary between Iraq and Kuwait
8.20	263	map	The Heartland Theory
8.21	266-267	map	Member States of the United Nations
8.22	268	map	European Supranationalism
8.23	270	photo	Hesdin, France (vegetable market with prices in euros)
8.24	271	photo	Brussels, Belgium (European Union umbrella)

Exercises for Chapter Tables and Figures

Look at Figure 8.13, Ethnic Mosaic of Eastern Europe. Compare Figure 8.13 to Figure 6.2, Languages of Europe. Compare the legends of the two maps and see if you can find any incongruencies. OK, since I am bringing this up there probably is an incongruency. But rather than give it away, I will let you look for it, like comparing two nearly identical pictures and trying to find what is different about them. If you find the incongruency, discuss whether or not it is an error, and if so, how such an error could be made.

Geographic Concepts

Geographic Concepts (Glossary of Terms)		
political geography	colonialism	territorial representation
state	scale	reapportionment
territoriality	capitalism	splitting
sovereignty	commodification	majority-minority districts
territorial integrity	core	gerrymandering boundary
Peace of Westphalia	periphery	geometric boundary
mercantilism	semiperiphery	physical-political boundary
nation	ability	heartland theory
nation-state	centripetal	critical geopolitics
democracy	centrifugal	unilateralism
multinational state	unitary	supranational organization
multistate nation	federal	
stateless nation	devolution	

Quiz for Geographic Concepts

Match the term with a definition.

1. ____ semi-periphery

2. ____ unilateralism

3. ____ devolution

4. ____ territoriality

5. ____ supranational organization

6. ____ sovereignty

7. ____ reapportionment

8. ____ stateless nation

9. ____ centrifugal

10. ____ critical geopolitics

11. ____ heartland theory

12. ____ multinational state

13. ____ centripetal

14. ____ nation-state

15. ____ capitalism

A. A venture involving three or more nation-states involving formal political, economic, and/or cultural cooperation to promote shared objectives.

B. A country's—or more local community's—sense of property and attachment toward its territory, as expressed by its determination to keep it inviolable and strongly defended.

C. A geopolitical hypothesis that any political power based in the heart of Eurasia could gain sufficient strength to eventually dominate the world.

D. Nation that does not have a state.

E. Economic model wherein people, corporations, and state produce goods and exchange them on the world market, with the goal of achieving profit.

F. State with more than one nation within its borders.

G. Theoretically, a recognized member of the modern state system possessing formal sovereignty and occupied by a people who see themselves as a single, united nation.

H. Places where core and periphery processes are both occurring; places that are exploited by the core but in turn exploit the periphery

I. The process whereby regions within a state demand and gain political strength and growing autonomy at the expense of the central government.

J. A principle of international relations that holds that final authority over social, economic, and political matters should rest with the legitimate rulers of independent states.

K. World order in which one state is in a position of dominance with allies following rather than joining the political decision-making process.

L. Process by which geopoliticians deconstruct and focus on explaining the underlying spatial assumptions and territorial perspectives of politicians.

M. Forces that tend to divide a country—such as internal religious, linguistic, ethnic, or ideological differences.

N.   Process by which representative districts are switched according to population shifts, so that each district encompasses approximately the same number of people.

O.   Forces that tend to unify a country—such as widespread commitment to a national culture, shared ideological objectives, and a common faith.

Chapter Related Internet Links

Learn More Online

About Country Studies Published by the United States Library of Congress
http://lcweb2.loc.gov/frd/cs/cshome.html

About the European Union
http://europa.eu.int/index_en.htm

About Nationalism
http://www.nationalismproject.org/

About Political Geography
http://www.politicalgeography.org

Watch It Online

Devolution
http://www.learner.org/resources/series180.html#program_descriptions
Click on Video On Demand. "Slovakia: New Sovereignty"

International Boundaries
http://www.learner.org/resources/series180.html#program_descriptions
click Video On Demand. "Boundaries and Borderlands"

Supranationalism and the European Union
http://www.learner.org/resources/series180.html#program_descriptions
click Video On Demand. "Strasbourg: Symbol of a United Europe"

Exercises for Chapter Related Internet Links

Watch the program "Strasbourg: Symbol of a United Europe." (about 12 minutes). Consider some of these questions:
- What is unique or special about the city of Strasbourg?
- What role does it play in the governance of the European Union?
- Discuss Strasbourg in terms of its site and situation.
- Contemplate the achievement of the European Union in terms of its porous borders; would such a model be good for North America?

- Should the NAFTA (http://en.wikipedia.org/wiki/NAFTA) countries have equally porous borders that allow for the free movement of people as well as goods and services?
- Can you imagine a future World Union or United States of Earth scenario (think of Star Trek) in which there would be one global currency and complete freedom to move from one region to any other?

APHG-Type Questions

Note: Be sure to take the online Self Tests on the Student Companion Site.
Check answer key at the end of the workbook.

Multiple Choice Questions

Type A: Basic Knowledge Questions

1. The League of Nations was created in 1919 as the first international organization that would include all nations of the world. Its success was dealt a serious blow by the failure of what country to join?
   A. Britain
   B. Russia
   C. the United States
   D. Canada
   E. China

2. One move by the old League of Nations that would have a critical impact in the second half of the twentieth century involved
   A. maritime boundaries
   B. refugee questions
   C. atmospheric boundaries
   D. mineral resources underlying two or more countries
   E. ignored global warming

3. The United Nations is not a world government, but in recent years individual states have asked the United Nations to do a number of different things, the most expensive of which is
   A. creating a common global currency
   B. monitoring elections
   C. providing for refugees
   D. setting maritime boundaries
   E. peacekeeping

4. The European Union's future expansion into the Muslim realm by the inclusion of _____ is highly controversial and strongly opposed by Greece.
   A. Saudi Arabia
   B. Bosnia
   C. Algeria
   D. Turkey
   E. Iraq

5. Sir Halford Mackinder developed what would become known as the *heartland theory* which suggested that interior Eurasia contained a critical "pivot area" that would generate a state capable of challenging for world domination. The key to the area according to Mackinder was
   A. natural protection
   B. distance
   C. natural resources
   D. Eastern Europe
   E. the Russian steppe

6. The movement of power from the central government to regional governments is referred to as
   A. revolution
   B. pluralism
   C. supranationalism
   D. devolution
   E. decentralization

7. The boundaries of independent African states were drawn at the Berlin Conference and were essentially drawn
   A. arbitrarily
   B. along ethnic lines
   C. along religious lines
   D. along ecological lines
   E. along linguistic lines

8. What ultimately proved to be the undoing of monarchical absolutism and its system of patronage during Europe's rebirth?
   A. the re-emergence of church power
   B. growing economic power of merchants
   C. an increasing population
   D. colonization
   E. labor shortage after the plague

9. Yugoslavia was a prime example of a
   A. multi-state nation
   B. nation-state
   C. stateless nation
   D. unitary state
   E. multi-nation state

10. The present number of countries and territories in the world is around
    A. 400
    B. 350
    C. 300
    D. 200
    E. 100

Type B: Application Questions

1. Robert Sack's view of human territorial behavior implies an expression of control over space and time. This control is closely related to the concept of
   A. nationhood
   B. colonialism
   C. sovereignty
   D. warfare
   E. hegemony

2. Nigeria is a state with a federal system of government. This fact is reflected in the adoption of _____ law in the states of the Muslim North.
   A. British Common
   B. Nigerian Federal
   C. sharia
   D. local tribal
   E. states' rights

3. In Italy, the Northern League's desire for independence was based on the economic difference between the northern Po region and the southern Mezzogiorno. These differences are attributed to
   A. regional ethnic differences
   B. religious differences between north and south
   C. core-periphery processes
   D. ecological differences
   E. respect for the rule of law

4. In 1943 Mackinder wrote about his concerns over the potential of Stalin's control of the countries of Eastern Europe. His views led to the development of the United States's containment policy and to the establishment of
   A. friendly relationships with China
   B. the United Nations
   C. N.A.T.O.
   D. the Berlin Wall
   E. COMECON

5. Listed among the challenges to the state in the twenty-first century are all the following EXCEPT
   A. nuclear weapons
   B. economic globalization
   C. increased cultural communication
   D. terrorism in the name of religion
   E. the United Nations

Free Response Question

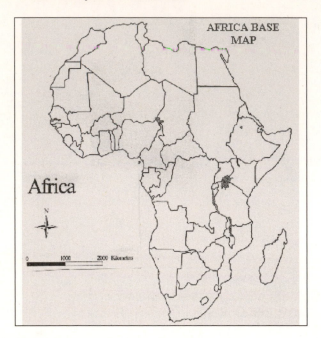

Africa has not been a peaceful continent in the post-colonial decades. Numerous wars within and between countries have lefts hundreds of thousands dead and millions displaced as refugees.

Give three examples of wars or conflict that have been (or are being) fought in Africa since 1990.

Explain the causes and consequences of those conflicts.

Discuss the reaction of the world community and the United Nations to those conflicts.

What are the main obstacles to peaceful coexistence between ethnic groups and states in Africa?

CHAPTER 9: URBAN GEOGRAPHY

Chapter Summary (from page 317)

The city is an ever changing cultural landscape, its layers reflecting grand plans by governments, impassioned pursuits by individuals, economic decisions by corporations, and processes of globalization. Geographers who study cities have a multitude of topics to examine. From gentrification to tear-downs, from favelas to McMansions, from spaces of production to spaces of consumption, from ancient walls to gated communities, cities have so much in common and yet each has its own pulse, its own feel, its own set of realities. The pulse of the city is undoubtedly created by the peoples and cultures who live there. For it is the people, whether working independently or as a part of a global corporation, who continuously create and re-create the city and its geography.

Key Questions

1. When and why did people start living in cities?
2. Where are cities located and why?
3. How are cities organized, and how do they function?
4. How do people make cities?
5. What role do cities play in globalization?

Field Notes

(274)   Straddling the Wall. The Berlin Wall separating east Berlin and West Berlin.

(286)   Rome, Italy. The Roman Forum.

(288)   Genoa, Italy. The historic importance of Genoa and Venice.

(290)   Duisburg, Germany. The Ruhr Valley industrial zone.

(292)   Broken Arrow, Oklahoma. Trade areas and vernacular regions.

(297)   Fort Worth, Texas. Gentrification of the downtown area.

(299)   Rio de Janeiro, Brazil. Hillside *favelas*.

(303)   Manila, Philippines. Garbage scavengers.

(304)   Cairo, Egypt. The urban landscape.

(305)   Cairo, Egypt. Minimally functional, and aesthetically non-descript housing projects.

(309)   Celebration, Florida. Walt Disney-designed new urbanist development.

Thinking Geographically

(290) Archaeologists have found that the houses in Indus River cities, such as Mohenjo-Daro and Harappa, were a uniform size: each house had access to a sewer system, and palaces were absent from the cultural landscape. Derive a theory as to why these conditions were present in these cities that had both a leadership class and a surplus of agricultural goods.

(294) Sketch a map of your city or town and the cities or towns nearby. Make a list of the kinds of goods and services available in each of these towns. Do the ideas about central places presented in this section of the chapter apply to your region?

(301) Employing the concepts defined in this section of the chapter, draw a model of the city with which you are most familiar. Label each section of the city accordingly. After reading through the models described in this section, determine which model best corresponds to the model you drew and hypothesize as to why it is so.

(314) Using the city you sketched in the last "Thinking Geographically" question, consider the concepts and processes introduced in this section of the chapter and explain how people and institutions created this city and the model you sketched.

(317) Thinking through the challenges to the state presented in Chapter 8, predict whether and under what circumstances world cities could replace states as the basic and most powerful form of political organization in the world.

Chapter Outline

A. When and Why Did People Start Living in Cities?
    1. The Hearths of Urbanization
    2. The Role of the Ancient City in Society
    3. Diffusion of Urbanization
    4. Greek Cities
    5. Roman Cities
    6. Urban growth After Greece and Rome
    7. Site and Situation during European Exploration
    8. The Second Urban Revolution
B. Where Are Cities Located and Why?
    1. Central Place Theory
    2. Hexagonal Hinterlands
    3. Central Places Today
C. How Are Cities Organized, and How Do They Function?
    1. Models of the City
    2. Modeling the North American City
    3. Modeling the Cities of the Global Periphery and Semiperiphery
    4. The Latin American City
    5. The African City
    6. The Southeast Asian City
D. How Do People Make Cities?
    1. Making Cities in the Global Periphery and Semiperiphery
    2. Making Cities in the Global Core
    3. Urban Sprawl and the New Urbanism
    4. Gated Communities
    5. Ethnic Neighborhoods in the European City
    6. Ethnic Neighborhoods in the Global Periphery and Semiperiphery City
E. What Role Do Cities Play In Globalization?
    Cities as Spaces of Consumption

Chapter Figures and Tables

Figure	Page	Type	Theme
9.1	274	photo	West Berlin, West Germany (view across Berlin Wall)
9.2	275	photo	Berlin Germany (East Germany guard tower)
9.3	278-279	map	Urban Population as a Percentage of the Total Population, by State
9.4	280	map	Hong Kong and Shenzhen, China
9.5	280	photo	Shenzhen, China
9.6	281	map	Five Hearths of Urbanization
9.7	282	map	Indus River Valley Urban Hearth
9.8	283	photo	Terracotta Warriors Guarding the Tomb of the Chinese Emperor Qin Shi Huang Di
9.9	283	map	Mayan and Aztec Civilizations
9.10	284	photo	Athens, Greece (the Acropolis and Parthenon)
9.11	285	photo	Athens, Greece (the Agora)
9.12	285	map	Roman Empire, c. 117 CE
9.13	286	photo	Rome, Italy (the Roman Forum)
9.14	286	photo	Nimes, France (Roman aqueduct)
9.15	287	photo	Altun Ha, Belize (Mayan pyramid)
9.16	288	photo	Genoa, Italy (cultural landscape)
9.17	289	map	Industrialized Regions of Europe, 1914
9.18	290	photo	Duisburg, Germany (rusting factory)
9.19	291	map	Map from commoncensus.org of cities in the United States
9.20	292	photo	Broken Arrow, Oklahoma (Green County Cycle City)
9.21	293	model	Christaller's Hierarchy of Settlements and their Service Areas
9.22	295	models	The Three Classical Models of Urban Structure
9.23	296	photo	Tyson's Corner, Virginia (example of an edge city)
9.24	297	photo	Fort Worth, Texas
9.25	297	model	Urban Realms Model
9.26	298	model	A New and Improved Model of the Latin American City Structure
9.27	299	photo	Rio de Janeiro, Brazil (favelas)
9.28	300	model	Model of the Subsaharan African City
9.29	300	model	Model of the Large Southeast Asian City
9.30	301	photo	Luanda, Angola (haves and have-nots)
9.31	302	photo	Tokyo, Japan (residential area)
9.32	303	photo	Manila, Philippines
9.33	303	photo	Temporary Shelter
9.34	304	photo	Cairo, Egypt (view of city)
9.35	305	photo	Cairo, Egypt (hastily built apartments)
9.36	306	photo	Hinsdale, Illinois (McMansions)
9.37	306	photo	Henderson, Nevada (suburb of Las Vegas)
T9.1	307	table	Top 20 Urban Sprawl Cities in the United States
9.38	309	photo	Celebration, Florida (master-planned community, residential street)
9.39	309	photo	Celebration, Florida (Sun Trust Bank)
9.40	310	photo	Gated Housing Community in Beijing, China
9.41	311	photo	St. Louis, Missouri (failed public housing project)
9.42	313	map	The Changing Character of Mumbai, India
9.43	314-315	map	World Cities: Alpha, Beta, and Gamma
9.44	317	photo	New York, New York (the New Amsterdam Theatre)

Exercises for Chapter Figures and Tables

In this chapter I count about twenty-five photographs of cities that include residential areas. Look over all of the photographs and think about where you would most like to live. Or imagine that you are working for a multinational corporation or a non-governmental organization (NGO) and you have your choice of overseas assignment, but you must choose based on what you see in these photographs of cities outside of the United States. Without critical analysis, just looking at the photographs, prioritize your top five choices.

Next look carefully at each photograph. Add to your knowledge of place by zooming in to the city using Google Earth (free download, but high speed connection really helpful). Look up the city on other web sites. Consider the city in terms of the social, economic and political characteristics of the country. Create a pros and cons table based on a more careful analysis of the different places. Once more prioritize your top five choices. Any differences?

Geographic Concepts

Geographic Concepts (Glossary of Terms)		
urban morphology	leadership class	Mesoamerica
city	first urban revolution	acropolis
urban	Mesopotamia	agora
agricultural village	Nile River Valley	site
agricultural surplus	Indus River Valley	Forum
social stratification	Huang He and Wei	situation
trade area	edge cities	gentrification
rank-size rule	urban realm	tear-downs
central place theory	Griffin-Ford model	McMansions
Sunbelt phenomenon	disamenity sector	urban sprawl
functional zonation	McGee model	new urbanism
zone	shantytowns	gated communities
central business district	zoning laws	informal economy
central city	redlining	world city
suburb	blockbusting	primate city
suburbanization	commercialization	spaces of consumption
concentric zone model		

Quiz for Geographic Concepts

Match the term with a definition.

1. _____ agricultural surplus

2. _____ central business district

3. _____ informal economy

4. _____ urban sprawl

5. _____ blockbusting

A. Unrestricted growth in many American urban areas of housing, commercial development, and roads over large expanses of land with little concern for urban planning.

B. Rivers in present-day China where chronologically the fourth urban hearth was established around 1500 BCE.

C. One of the two components, together with agricultural surplus, which enables the formation of cities; the differentiation of society into classes based on wealth, power, production and prestige.

6. ____ shantytowns

7. ____ Mesopotamia

8. ____ Huang He and Wei

9. ____ urban morphology

10. ____ functional zonation

11. ____ central place theory

12. ____ site

13. ____ first urban revolution

14. ____ gentrification

15. ____ situation

D. The external locational attributes of a place; its relative location or regional position with reference to other nonlocal places.

E. The physical attributes of a place, including its absolute location, its spatial character and physical setting.

F. Economic activity that is neither taxed nor monitored by a government, and is not included in that government's gross national product (GNP).

G. The study of the physical form and structure of urban places.

H. The division of a city into different regions for certain purposes, like housing or manufacturing.

I. The rehabilitation of deteriorated, often abandoned housing of low income inner-city residents.

J. Proposes to explain how and where central places in the urban hierarchy should be functionally and spatially distributed with respect to one another.

K. Rapid change in the racial composition of residential blocks in American cities that occurs when real estate agents stir up fears of neighborhood decline after encouraging people of color to move to previously white neighborhoods.

L. The downtown heart of a central city, marked by high land values, a concentration of business and commerce, and the clustering of the tallest building.

M. The innovation of the city, which occurred independently in five separate hearths.

N. Region of great cities located between the Tigris and Euphrates Rivers; the first urban hearth dating to about 3500 BCE.

O. Unplanned slum development on the margins of cities, dominated by crude dwellings made mostly of scrap materials.

Chapter Related Internet Links

Learn More Online

About Celebration, Florida
http://www.celebrationfl.com/

About the Congress for the New Urbanism
http://www.cnu.org

About Globalization and World Cities
http://www.lut.ac.uk/gawc/index.html

About Opposition to Urban Sprawl
http://www.sierraclub.org/sprawl/

About Seaside, Florida
http://www.seasidefl.com/

Watch It Online

About Berlin (1)
http://www.learner.org/resources/series180.html#program_descriptions
Click on Video On Demand. "Berlin: United We Stand"

About Berlin (1)
http://www.learner.org/resources/series85.html#program_descriptions
click Video On Demand. "Berlin: Changing Center of a Changing Europe"

About Sprawl in Chicago
http://www.learner.org/resources/series180.html
click Video On Demand. "Chicago: Farming on the Edge"

Exercises for Chapter Related Internet Links

Learn about urban sprawl in the Chicago region by watching the program: "Chicago: Farming on the Edge." Write down the names of the edge cities mentioned in the video. Buy a North American Road Atlas (UniversalMap, AAA, or Rand McNally) and locate those cities on the Chicago and Vicinity map. Consider some of these questions:

- What changes in American society have made urban sprawl possible?
- What are the consequences of lost farmland regionally, nationally and globally as other countries also lose land to urban growth?
- Contemplate the time it takes for nature to produce good soil versus the time it takes to build a city.
- Why are so many farmers in the near hinterlands of big cities willing to sell the family farm?
- Discuss this phenomenon in terms of post-industrial transformation.
- What is implied by the notion of "back to our roots," and how "real" is it?

- Do you feel there is a moral imperative to preserve the way of life and quality of life of small-town, rural America?

APHG-Type Questions

Note: Be sure to take the online Self Tests on the Student Companion Site.
Check answer key at the end of the workbook.

Multiple Choice Questions

Type A: Basic Knowledge.

1. Ethnic neighborhoods in European cities reflect migrants from
   A. Eastern Europe
   B. poor Mediterranean Europe
   C. former colonies
   D. Latin America
   E. gypsy communities

2. Segregation in the United States was reinforced by the financial practice known as
   A. redlining
   B. community block grants
   C. land use zoning
   D. tax increment financing
   E. microcredit

3. In core area cities the practice of buying up and rehabilitating deteriorating housing which resulted in the raising of housing values and a social change in neighborhoods is called
   A. public housing
   B. gentrification
   C. white flight
   D. urban renewal
   E. revitalization

4. The huge influx of population from rural to urban areas in peripheral or semi-peripheral areas (less developed countries) find housing in
   A. public housing
   B. edge cities
   C. deteriorating CBD's
   D. high density apartments
   E. shantytowns

5. A structural element of many Latin American cities, the disamenity sector, is illustrated by the
   A. mall
   B. *barrios* or *favelas*
   C. commercial spine
   D. industrial park
   E. presence of Chinese

6. Which of the following is BOTH the least urbanized AND the most rapidly urbanizing realm of the world?
    A. Middle America
    B. Africa south of the Sahara
    C. East Asia
    D. South Asia
    E. the Middle East

7. In Southeast Asian cities the *alien commercial zone* is dominated by
    A. American corporations
    B. Europeans
    C. Chinese
    D. Lebanese traders
    E. extraterrestrials

8. The relative location of a city refers to its
    A. site
    B. situation
    C. genealogy of development
    D. approximate latitude and longitude
    E. physical characteristics

9. The *manufacturing* city (post Industrial Revolution) first emerged in
    A. the British Midlands
    B. central Italy
    C. the French coastal region
    D. the Ruhr
    E. Appalachia

10. In which of the following regions did urbanization develop first?
    A. Mesopotamia
    B. Nile River Valley
    C. Indus River Valley
    D. China
    E. Mesoamerica

Type B: Application

1. The layout of a city, the physical form and structure, is referred to as
    A. zoning
    B. urban grid
    C. city plan
    D. urban street pattern
    E. urban morphology

2. A hinterland reveals the _____ of each settlement.
    A. total population
    B. working population
    C. economic reach
    D. aggregate purchasing power
    E. quality of agricultural land

3. Paris and Mexico City are many times larger than the second-ranked city in their respective countries. Their disproportionate size illustrates
    A. the concept of the primate city
    B. the fact that capital cities are always very large
    C. the rank-size rule
    D. the effects of suburbanization
    E. urban power structures

4. The *multiple nuclei model* of urban structure developed by Harris and Ullman arose from the idea that _____ was losing its dominant position in the metropolitan city.
    A. the CBD
    B. the inner city
    C. public transportation
    D. the suburb
    E. private housing

5. If cities in the poorer parts of the world share a common characteristic, it may result from
    A. an absence of enforced zoning regulations
    B. a total lack of industry
    C. acute water shortages
    D. poor public transportation
    E. civil unrest

Free Response Question

Discuss the central place theory of urban systems advanced by Christaller. Describe the following features of the theory: central place, trade area, and hexagonal hinterlands. What assumptions did Christaller make when formulating the theory? Give one example of an area where his theory seems to explain the distribution of cities.

CHAPTER 10: DEVELOPMENT

Chapter Summary (from page 347)

The idea of economic development is relatively new; it implies a sense of progressively improving a country's economic situation that gained a sense of normalcy after the Industrial Revolution. Before that time, differences in economic wealth among countries were not as well known or as exaggerated. Geographers recognize the structures of the world-economy, seeing how these structures limit the ability of all states to reach the same level of economic development. Geographers also recognize that economic development in a single place is based on a multitude of factors, including core and periphery processes, the link the place plays in commodity chains, the efficacy of government, the presence of disease, the lack of nutrition, the presence of foreign debt, the success or failure of government programs, and the influence of nongovernmental programs. Geographers also realize that all these processes and others are operating concurrently across scales, making a country's journey across economic development indubitably much more difficult than climbing a ladder.

Key Questions

1. How do you define and measure development?
2. How does geographical situation affect development?
3. What are the barriers to and the costs of development?
4. How do political and economic institutions influence uneven development within states?

Field Notes

(319)   Geography, Trade and Development

(322)   Sukabumi, West Java. Migrant women workers in Indonesia.

(334)   Buenos Aires, Argentina. Development problems.

(343)   New Orleans, Louisiana. Conditions after Hurricane Katrina.

(346)   Port Gentile, Gabon. Consequences of the discovery of oil.

Thinking Geographically

(326) Is the idea of economic development inherently Western? If the West (North America and Europe) were not encouraging the "developing world" to "develop," how would people in the regions of the "developing world" think about their own economies?

(328) Compare and contrast Rostow's ladder of development with Wallerstein's three-tier structure of the world-economy as models for understanding a significant economic shift that has occurred in the place where you grew up. What are the advantages and disadvantages of the two models?

(342) Think of a trip you have made to a poorer area of the country or a poorer region of the world. Describe how your experience in the place as a tourist was fundamentally different from the everyday lives of the people who live in the place.

(346) Take an item of clothing out of your closet and, using the Internet, try to trace the commodity chain of production. What steps did the item go through before reaching you? Consider the types of economic processes that were operating at each step and consider the roles governments and international political regimes played along the way.

Chapter Outline

A. How Do You Define and Measure Development?
1. Gross national Income
2. Development Models
B. How Does Geography Affect Development?
1. Dependency Theory
2. Geography and Context
C. What Are The Barriers To And The Costs Of Development?
1. Barriers to Economic Development
a. Social Conditions
b. Disease
c. Foreign Debt
d. Political Instability
2. Costs of Economic Development
a. Industrialization
b. Agriculture
c. Tourism
D. How do political and economic institutions influence uneven development within states?
1. The Role of Governments
2. Islands of Development
3. Creating Growth in the Periphery of the Periphery

Chapter Figures and Tables

Figure	Page	Type	Theme
10.1	319	photo	Timbuktu, Mali. Dirt streets reflect impoverishment.
10.2	322	photo	Sukabumi, West Java (migrant women workers from Indonesia)
10.3	323	graph	Differences in Communications Connectivity Around the World
10.4	324-325	map	Dependency Ratio by Country
10.5	326	graph	Rostow's Ladder of Development
10.6	327	photo	San Salvador, El Salvador (fruit juice vendor)
10.7	330-331	map	Human Development Index
10.8	332-332	map	External debt service as a percentage of exports of goods and services for low-and middle income economies, 2006
10.9	334	photo	Buenos Aires, Argentina (financial crisis of 2001)
10.10	336-337	map	Global Distribution of Malaria Transmission Risk, 2003
10.11	338	photo	Tamolo, India (Nicobar Islands after tsunami)
10.12	339	map	Export Processing Zones by Country
10.13	340-341	map	Areas Threatened by Desertification
10.14	343	photo	Destroyed House in the Lower Ninth Ward, New Orleans
10.15	345	photo	Putrajaya, Malaysia (new capital city)
10.16	346	photo	Port Gentile, Gabon (oil storage tank)
10.17	347	photo	Bwindi, Uganda. Women walk by a microcredit agency that has facilitated economic development in the town

Exercise for Chapter Figure and Tables

Figure 10.4, Dependency Ratio, maps one of many social welfare measurements that are used to imply a country's level of development. The Dependency Ratio is a measure of the number of dependents, young and old, that each 100 employed people must support. A quick glance at the map reveals the high dependency ratio for countries in Africa, Southwest Asia, South Asia and parts of Southeast Asia.

- Describe how a population pyramid (textbook page 56) might look for a country with a high dependency ratio. Then look at the actual pyramid for a selection of countries at: http://www.census.gov/ipc/www/idbpyr.html
- The map indicates that there are several countries we would normally think of as Less Developed (e.g., Kazakhstan, Chile, Indonesia), yet their dependency ratio is the same as the United States and Western Europe. How can that be explained?
- If a low dependency ratio is a good indicator of level of development, explain why Eastern European countries have a lower ratio than the clearly more developed Western European countries.

Geographic Concepts

Geographic Concepts (Glossary of Terms)		
commodity chain	neo-colonialism	malaria
developing	structuralist theory	export processing zones
gross national product (GNP)	dependency theory	maquiladoras
	dollarization	special economic zones
gross domestic product (GDP)	world-systems theory	North American Free Trade Agreement (NAFTA)
	three-tier structure	
gross national income (GNI)	Millennium Development Goals	desertification
per capita GNI	trafficking	island of development
formal economy	structural adjustment loans	nongovernmental organizations (NGOs)
informal economy		
modernization model	neoliberalism	microcredit program
context	vectored diseases	

Quiz for Geographic Concepts

Match the term with a definition.

1. ____ structural adjustment loan

2. ____ developing

3. ____ formal economy

4. ____ nongovernmental organization

5. ____ world systems theory

A. With respect to a country, making progress in technology, production, and socioeconomic welfare.

B. Loans granted by international financial institutions such as the World Bank and International Monetary Fund in exchange for certain economic and governmental reforms in that country.

C. The total value of all goods and services produced by a country's economy in a given year, and includes all goods and services produced by corporations and individuals of a country whether or not they are located in the country.

6. ____ microcredit program

7. ____ neocolonialism

8. ____ GNP

9. ____ modernization model

10. ____ export processing zones

11. ____ per capita GNI

12. ____ structuralist theory

13. ____ maquiladoras

14. ____ dependency theory

15. ____ NAFTA

D. The entrenchment of the colonial order, such as trade and investment, under a new guide.

E. The term given to zones in northern Mexico with factories supplying manufactured goods to the U.S. market; low wage workers assemble imported components and export finished goods.

F. A general term for a model of economic development that treats economic disparities among countries or regions as the result of historically derived power relations within the global economic system.

G. International organizations that operate outside the formal political arena but that are nonetheless influential in spearheading international initiatives on social, economic and environmental issues.

H. Zones established by many countries in the periphery or semi-periphery where they offer favorable tax, regulatory, and trade arrangements to attract foreign trade and investment.

I. Originated by Immanuel Wallerstein and illuminated by his three-tier structure, proposing that social change in the developing world is inextricably linked to the economic activities of the developed world.

J. Model of economic development most closely associated with the work of economist Walter Rostow; maintains that all countries go through five interrelated stages of development.

K. Agreement entered into by Canada, the United States and Mexico in December 1992, and which took effect on Jan. 1, 1994, to eliminate the barriers to trade in goods and services between the countries.

L. A structuralist theory based on the idea that certain types of political and economic relations between countries and regions of the world have created arrangements that both control and limit the extent to which regions can develop.

M. The legal economy that is taxed and monitored by a government and is included in a government's Gross National Product.

N. Programs that provide small loans to poor people, especially women, to encourage development of small business.

O. The Gross National Income of a country divided by its population.

Chapter Related Internet Links

Exercises for Chapter Related Internet Links

After watching the program "Gabon: Sustainable Resources," discuss the situation in Gabon in terms of:

- primary economic activities
- non-renewable resources
- income inequality
- sustainable development

Some other questions you might want to consider:

- the primary primary resources (a little play on words) that sustain the economy
- why the export of primary commodities is "inefficient"
- the magnitude of the oil exporting economy in Gabon
- living conditions in the capital of Libreville
- images in the video of Gabon's informal economy

APHG-Type Questions

Note: Be sure to take the online Self Tests on the Student Companion Site.
Check answer key at the end of the workbook.

Multiple Choice Questions

Type A: Basic Knowledge.

1. Port Gentile, Gabon was built by
   A. an ancient Gabonese civilization
   B. British colonizers.
   C. European oil companies
   D. migrants fleeing the Congo
   E. Dubai orts International

2. Twenty thousand nongovernmental organizations (NGOs) in Bangladesh constitute what can be called
   A. a parallel state
   B. colonial enclaves
   C. development islands
   D. subversive zones
   E. special economic zones (SEZs)

3. Many tourist areas in peripheral regions are beach resorts. In 2004 Thailand's beach resort areas were ravaged by
   A. cockroach infestations
   B. volcanic ash
   C. prolonged drought
   D. terror attacks
   E. a tsunami

4. Mexico has established export processing zones with special tax, trade and regulatory arrangements for foreign firms. This phenomena is referred to as
   A. maquiladoras
   B. haciendas
   C. border cities
   D. NAFTA zones
   E. free trade area

5. High levels of development can be determined by measurement of access to railways, roads, airline connections, telephones, radio and television, etc. These are collectively referred to as
   A. infrastructure
   B. dependency measures
   C. formal economy
   D. commodity connections
   E. media links

6. Which is NOT among the five stages of Rostow's development model?
   A. traditional
   B. take-off
   C. high-mass consumption
   D. collapse-decline
   E. drive to maturity

7. Even if the Gross National Product (GNP) per capita index is used to measure the well-being of a country, it will fail to show
   A. growth in secondary industries (manufacturing)
   B. the distribution of wealth
   C. growth within tertiary industries (services)
   D. growth within primary industries (mining, forestry, agriculture, fishing)
   E. change in the economy over time

8. The principal structuralist alternative to Rostow's model of economic development is known as
   A. the "takeoff" model
   B. the liberal model
   C. the modernization model
   D. dependency theory
   E. grass roots activism

9. The continuation of economic dependence even after political independence is referred to as
   A. precondition to take-off
   B. modernization model
   C. post-colonialism
   D. independence movement
   E. neocolonialism

10. Which of the following has the highest per capita GNP?
   A. Japan
   B. United States
   C. European Union
   D. Canada
   E. Saudi Arabia

Type B: Application Questions

1. Which of the following is NOT associated with core production processes?
   A. technology
   B. low-wage labor
   C. education
   D. research and development
   E. modern cities

2. Which does NOT make up a portion of Colombia's GNP?
   A. professional sports franchises
   B. tourism
   C. coffee production
   D. drug trafficking
   E. flower exports

3. A large component of survival in countries with low per capita GNP is
   A. foreign aid
   B. the sale of resources
   C. the informal economy
   D. tourism
   E. prostitution

4. Subsistence forms of agriculture in peripheral areas produce little in the way of
   A. protein
   B. grain crops
   C. root crops
   D. foodstuffs
   E. useful fibers

112

5. A look at the maps of Nigeria, Pakistan and Brazil would show that when governments established new post-colonial capitals, they moved away from
   A. swamps
   B. deserts
   C. areas of ethnic discord
   D. internal regions
   E. coastal port areas

Free Response Question

Country	RNI %	IMR	LEB	GNI/C	PD/mile^2
A	2.9	81	44	1,220	132
B	-0.1	4.0	77	20,730	256
C	0.1	2.8	82	30,040	876
D	1.4	8	77	21,000	143
E	1.9	80	52	1,680	774
F	-0.3	57	35	8,920	7
G	0.5	5	77	20,400	1,260
H	0.3	5.4	80	30,660	8
I	0.3	3.2	80	38,550	37

source of data: 2005 World Population Data Sheet (Population Reference Bureau)

RNI %: rate of natural increase
IMR: infant mortality rate
LEB: life expectancy at birth
GNI/C: gross national income per capita (PPP)
PD/mile^2: population density per square mile

Of the above nine countries, three can be classified as More Developed, three as Middle Developed, and three as Less Developed.

Based on the demographic data in the table, match the letters of the countries with the level of development.

Discuss which variables are the most useful and least useful in determining level of development.

Indicate any anomalies, that is, data for a country that seems to be counter intuitive.

Based on your knowledge of the Rostow Take-Off Model of development, at what stage of development would these countries be?

CHAPTER 11: AGRICULTURE

Chapter Summary (from page 359)

Agricultural production has changed drastically since the First Agricultural Revolution. Today, agricultural products, even perishable ones, are shipped around the world, and agriculture has industrialized and spurred the growth of agribusiness. A major commonality between ancient agriculture and modern agriculture remains: the need to change. Trial and error were the norms of early plant and animal domestication. And today, trial and error are still the norm, as agriculture in the globalized economy is complicated by new technologies, genetically engineered crops, cultural change, government involvement, and the lasting impacts of history.

Key Questions

1. What is agriculture, and where did agriculture begin?
2. How did agriculture change with industrialization?
3. What imprint does agriculture make on the cultural landscape?
4. What is the global pattern of agriculture and agribusiness?

Field Notes

(349)   Changing Greens. Presho, South Dakota. Soybeans growing in the semiarid ranchlands of western South Dakota.

(358)   Animal domestication experiment station, Nairobi, Kenya.

(364)   Gambia. Women and rural development in Subsaharan Africa.

Thinking Geographically

(360) Settling down in one place, a rising population, and the switch to agriculture are interrelated occurrences in human history. Hypothesize which of these three happened first, second, and third and explain why.

(364) Genetically engineered crops are yielding some ethical problems. In the semi-periphery and periphery, farmers typically keep seeds from crops so that they can plant the seeds the next year. Companies that produce genetically engineered seeds do not approve of this process; generally, they want farmers to purchase new seeds each year. Using the concepts of scale and jumping scale, determine the ethical questions in this debate.

(370) Think of an agricultural region you have either visited or seen from an airplane. Describe the imprint of agriculture on the landscape and consider what the cultural landscape tells you about how agriculture is produced in this region and how production has changed over time.

Chapter Outline

A. What Is Agriculture, and Where Did Agriculture Begin?
    1. Hunting, Gathering, and Fishing
    2. Terrain and Tools
    3. The First Agricultural Revolution
    4. Domestication of Animals
    5. Hunter-Gatherers in the Modern World

Chapter Figures and Tables

Figure	Page	Type	Theme
11.1	349	photo	Presho, South Dakota (soybeans)
11.2	351	map	Acres of Land Certified for Organic Agricultural Production in the United States, 2002
11.3	354	map	The Fertile Crescent
11.4	355	map	World Areas of Agricultural Innovations
T11.1	356	table	Chief Source Regions of Important Crop Plant Domestication
11.5	358	photo	Nairobi, Kenya (animal domestication)
11.6	359	map	World Regions of Primary Subsistence Agriculture
11.7	361	model	Von Thünen's Model
11.8	364	photo	Gambia (irrigated rice project)
11.9	365	photo	Garden City, Iowa (effect of the township-and-range system)
11.10	366	map	Dominant Land Survey Patterns in the United States
11.11	367	photo	Burgundy, France (agricultural landscape)
11.12	368	models	Village Forms
11.13	369	photo	Siem Reap, Cambodia (stilt village in Mekong basin)
11.14	369	photo	Winthrop, Minnesota (modern American farm)
11.15	370	photo	Dunedin, New Zealand (refrigerated containers)
11.16	372-373	map	World Climates (Köppen-Geiger)
11.17	374-375	map	World Agriculture
11.18	376	photo	Las Colinas Cooperative, El Salvador
11.19	380	map	Farming on the Edge: High Quality Farmland in the Path of Development, 2003

Exercise for Chapter Related Figures and Tables

Look at Figure 11.9, an oblique aerial photo of Garden City, Iowa and the surrounding farmland.

Use Google Earth to zoom in on Iowa (be sure to check the Roads and Borders layers). At what altitude (bottom right) do you begin to see the regular grid pattern imposed on the landscape? Zoom in closer and watch the pattern of roads and boundaries emerge. Describe the roads and boundaries.

Find Garden City, Iowa (42° 14.7' N 93° 23.8' W) on Google Earth or TopoUSA (or any other mapping software you might have access to).

Read about the Land Ordinance Act of 1785 and the township-and-range system of land surveying.

With all of this information, look at the Figure 11.9 again. Can you identify section boundaries in the photo?

Geographic Concepts

Geographic Concepts (Glossary of Terms)		
organic agriculture	subsistence agriculture	metes and bound system
agriculture	shifting cultivation	longlot survey system
primary economic activity	slash-and-burn agriculture	primogeniture
secondary economic activity	Second Agricultural	commercial agriculture
tertiary economic activity	Revolution	monoculture
quaternary economic activity	von Thünen model	Köppen climatic classification
quinary economic activity	Third Agricultural Revolution	system
plant domestication	Green Revolution	climatic regions
root crops	genetically modified	plantation agriculture
seed crops	organisms	luxury crops
First Agricultural Revolution	rectangular survey system	livestock ranching
animal domestication	township and range system	Mediterranean agriculture
		agribusiness

Quiz for Geographic Concepts

Match the term with a definition.

1. _____ township and range

2. _____ primary economic activity

3. _____ First Agricultural Revolution

4. _____ agribusiness

5. _____ Green Revolution

6. _____ metes and bounds

A.   System in which the eldest son in the family inherits all of a dying parent's land.

B.   A rectangular land division scheme designed by Thomas Jefferson to disperse settlers evenly across farmlands of the U.S interior.

C.   Service sector industries concerned with the collection, processing and manipulation of information and capital.

D.   Economic activity involving the processing of raw materials and their transformation into finished industrial products; the manufacturing sector.

7. ____ subsistence agriculture

8. ____ quaternary economic activity

9. ____ von Thünen model

10. ____ secondary economic activity

11. ____ longlot survey system

12. ____ Mediterranean agriculture

13. ____ shifting cultivation

14. ____ Third Agricultural Revolution

15. ____ primogeniture

E. Specialized farming that occurs only in areas where the dry-summer, wet-winter climate prevails.

F. Dating back 10,000 years, a time and place that achieved plant and animal domestication.

G. The recently successful development of higher-yield, fast growing varieties of rice and other cereals in certain developing countries.

H. Economic activity concerned with the direct extraction of natural resources from the environment—such as mining, fishing and agriculture.

I. Currently in progress, its principal orientation is the development of Genetically Modified Organisms.

J. Cultivation of crops in tropical forest clearings in which the forest vegetation has been removed by cutting and burning.

K. Explains the location of agricultural activities in a commercial, profit-making economy; process of spatial competition allocates various farming activities into rings around a central market city.

L. A system of land surveying east of the Appalachian Mountains that relies on descriptions of land ownership and natural features such as streams and trees.

M. Self-sufficient agriculture that is small scale and low technology and emphasizes food production for local consumption, not trade.

N. Distinct regional approach to land surveying found in the Canadian Maritimes, parts of Quebec, Louisiana, and Texas whereby land is divided into narrow parcels stretching back from rivers, roads or canals.

O. General term for the businesses that provide the vast array of good and services that support the agricultural industry.

Chapter Related Internet Links

Guns, Germs, and Steel
http://www.pbs.org/gunsgermssteel/

Loss of Agricultural Lands to Suburbanization in Chicago
http://www.learner.org/resources/series180.html#program_descriptions
Click on Video On Demand for program 24

Russia's Farming Revolution
http://www.learner.org/resources/series180.html#program_descriptions
Click on Video On Demand Program 7: Vologda: Russian Farming in Flux

Sustainable Agriculture in India
http://www.learner.org/resources/series180.html#program_descriptions
Click on Video On Demand for program 17

Exercises for Chapter Related Internet Links

Watch the video program: Vologda: Russian Farming in Flux.
- In what ways is farming in Vologda similar and dissimilar to farming in America?
- What are the biggest challenges relative to the physical environment?
- What are the biggest challenges relative to social and economic conditions?
- What demographic cohort tends to leave the farming lifestyle, perhaps to migrate to cities in search of work?
- Discuss the transition from collective agriculture to a market economy.

APHG-Type Questions

Note: Be sure to take the online Self Tests on the Student Companion Site.
Check answer key at the end of the workbook.

Multiple Choice Questions

Type A: Basic Knowledge

1. In recent years, many wooded areas in _____ have been deforested to provide beef for hamburgers for fast-food chains in the United States.
   A. East and South Asia
   B. West Africa
   C. East Africa
   D. Central and South America
   E. Canada

2. Rice cultivation in Southeast Asia is largely a _____ activity.
   A. part-time
   B. commercial
   C. government
   D. mechanized
   E. subsistence

3. Twenty-five percent of world sugar production takes place outside of the tropical plantation region (U.S.A., Western Europe, Russia) and is produced from
   A. genetically-modified, cold-tolerant sugar cane
   B. sugar beets
   C. wood cellulose
   D. artificial food chemical processes
   E. corn syrup

4. Rubber trees were first tapped in
   A. eastern Venezuela
   B. northern South America's Amazon Basin
   C. Malaya
   D. Indonesia
   E. Africa's tropical rain forest

5. Coffee was domesticated in Ethiopia. Today, 70% of production is in
   A. Southeast Asia
   B. South Asia
   C. East Africa
   D. Middle and South America
   E. North America

6. Fair trade coffee buyers certify that _____ % of the retail price of their coffee goes to the coffee growers.
   A. 80
   B. 100
   C. 40
   D. 5
   E. 15

7. The rectangular land division scheme in the United States adopted after the American Revolution is quite unique. Its correct name is
   A. long-lot system
   B. metes and bounds system
   C. mile-grid system
   D. Franklin's system
   E. township-and-range system

8. According to Spencer and Thomas, each agricultural hearth was associated with a local grouping of plants. For example, taro, yams, and bananas are associated with the _____ hearth.
   A. Meso-American
   B. Southeast Asian
   C. Southwest Asian
   D. Ethiopia-East African
   E. Amazonian

9. A form of tropical subsistence agriculture in which fields are rotated after short periods of crop production is
   A. subsistence rice cultivation
   B. subsistence wheat cultivation
   C. shifting cultivation
   D. nomadic herding
   E. slash-and-burn

10. Bio-genetic engineering now allows the growing of new plant strains in more arid regions of the Plains States to meet the demand of the _____ industry.
    A. cattle feed
    B. bio-diesel fuel
    C. tofu/organic food
    D. grain export
    E. famine aid

Type B: Application Questions

1. Which is NOT an example of a primary economic activity?
   A. corn flake production
   B. iron ore production
   C. lobster fishing
   D. forestry
   E. petroleum extraction

2. In areas of shifting cultivation the population
   A. increases significantly
   B. cannot have a high density
   C. must be large enough to provide surplus labor
   D. never lives in permanent settlements
   E. practices an unsustainable form of agriculture

3. Colonial powers would make subsistence farmers
   A. grow cash crops only
   B. farm on plantations in addition to farming their own land
   C. grow cash crops in addition to food crops the farmer needed to survive
   D. buy commercial fertilizer at fixed prices
   E. leave the land to work in factories

4. Before the intervention of Europeans, the societies practicing subsistence farming were quite equal because
   A. populations were small
   B. the farmers did not live in villages or other settlements
   C. land was held in communal ownership
   D. money was equally divided
   E. the form of religion, animism, emphasizes egalitarianism

5. Poorer countries, producing such cash crops as sugar,
    A. set the market price themselves
    B. rapidly change to a different cash crop when commodity prices decline
    C. plant less in order to drive up the prices
    D. cooperate with each other to determine global prices and demand
    E. are at the mercy of the purchasing countries that set the prices

Free Response Question

Describe the township-and-range system.

1. When did the system come into being?

2. Beginning with an initial point, describe how the lines are drawn and the areas labeled.

3. What does this nomenclature refer to: NW¼NE¼SE¼NW¼

CHAPTER 12: INDUSTRY AND SERVICE

Chapter Summary (from page 408)

The Industrial Revolution transformed the world economically, politically, and socially. Many of the places where industrialization first took hold have since become deindustrialized, both with the relocation of manufacturing plants and with the outsourcing of steps of production process domestically and offshore. With changing economics, places change. Some now look like ghost towns, serving merely as a reminder that industrialization took place there. Others have booming economies and thriving towns, having kept industry or having successfully cultivated a service economy. Other places are still redefining themselves. In the next chapter, we consider another lasting effect of industrialization and deindustrialization: environmental change.

Key Questions

1. Where did the Industrial Revolution begin, and how did it diffuse?
2. How do location theories explain historical patterns of industrialization?
3. How has industrial production changed, and with what geographic consequences?
4. Where are the major industrial belts in the world today and why?
5. What is the service economy, and where are services concentrated?

Field Notes

(382) Branding the Backboard, Skopje, Macedonia. The Nike "swoosh" is everywhere.

(388) Rouen, France. The industrial and agricultural heart of France.

(403) Beijing, China. The old is swept away in favor of the new.

(406) Fayetteville, Arkansas. The changing urban/economic landscape.

Thinking Geographically

(388) Examine the map of diffusion of the Industrial Revolution into Europe and determine what other characteristics (aside from presence of coal) were necessary for industrialization to take hold in these regions.

(398) Think of an industrial area near the place where you live, either an industrial park or a major conglomeration of industries. Drive through the area or look online or in the phone book to see what industries are located there. Consider the models of industrial location described in this section of the chapter and determine whether any of the models help explain the mix of industries present in this place.

(402) Think about a cutting-edge, high-technology product that is still quite expensive to purchase and not yet broadly used (perhaps something you have read about but not even seen). Using the Internet, determine where this product is manufactured and assess why the product is manufactured there. Hypothesize which countries production will shift to and how long it will take for production costs (and the price of the product) to decrease substantially.

(404) How does a place change when deindustrialization occurs? Consider a place that has experienced deindustrialization, and research recent news articles on the Internet to find out how the economy of the place has changed since the loss of industry. What has happened to the place and its economy?

(408) What majors are most popular at your college or university? Consider what service/high-technology corridors may already exist near your college or university. Propose a new service/high-technology corridor for your region based on what your college/university has to offer the industry. Where might it be located? What are the advantages and disadvantages of different possible locations?

Chapter Outline

A. Where Did the Industrial Revolution Begin, and How Did It Diffuse?
   1. The Industrial Revolution
   2. Diffusion to Mainland Europe
B. How Do Location Theories Explain Industrial Location?
   1. Weber's Model
   2. Hotelling's Model
   3. Lösch's Model
   4. Major Industrial Regions of the World Before 1950
      a. Western and Central Europe
         The Manufacturing Belts of Europe
      b. North America
         The American Manufacturing Belt
      c. The Former Soviet Union
         The Ukraine Manufacturing Belt
      d. Eastern Asia
         The Japanese Manufacturing Belt
C. How Has Industrial Production Changed?
   1. Televisions—the Core, the Semi-Periphery, and the Periphery
   2. New Influences on the Geography of Manufacturing
      a. Importance of Transportation in Industrial Location
      b. Importance of Regional and Global Trade Agreements
      c. Importance of Energy in Industrial Location
D. Where Are The Major Industrial Belts In The World Today And Why?
   Eastern China
E. What Is The Service Economy, And Where Are Services Concentrated?
   1. Geographical Dimensions of the Service Economy
      New Influences on Location
   2. High Technology Corridors

Chapter Figures and Tables

Figure	Page	Type	Theme
12.1	382	photo	Skopje, Macedonia (Nike "swoosh")
12.2	385	map	Capital Flows into Europe during Colonialism
12.3	386	photo	Ironbridge, England (world's first bridge made of cast iron)
12.4	386	map	The Origins of the Industrial Revolution
12.5	387	map	Diffusion of the Industrial Revolution
12.6	388	photo	Rouen, France (major industrial complex)
12.7	390	graph	Economic Influences on Business Location

T12.1	391	table	Top 20 Crude Steel Producers
12.8	392	map	Major Industrial Regions of Europe
12.9	393	map	Major Deposits of Fossil Fuels in North America
12.10	394	map	Major Manufacturing Regions of North America
12.11	396	map	Major Manufacturing Regions of Russia
12.12	397	map	Major Manufacturing Regions of East Asia
T12.2	401	table	World's Largest Oil Producers
12.13	403	photos	Beijing, China (old and new housing)
12.14	405	photo	Liverpool, England (industrial decline, abandoned streets)
12.15	406	photo	Fayetteville, Arkansas (Procter & Gamble)
12.16	408	photo	Plano-Richardson, Texas

Exercise for Chapter Figures and Tables

Let's look at a table this time, Table 12.1, Top Crude Steel Producers. Create a table with five or six columns, by hand, or using a word processing application, or better yet a spreadsheet program like Excel.

One column will be the countries in Table 12.1, another the steel tonnage. Then use the CIA World Fact Book (http://www.cia.gov/cia/publications/factbook/) to look up these countries. Choose some of the variables to fill in additional columns, things like the size of the country, its population, its per capita GDP, and others you think might be relevant.

Do you see any correlation between these additional variables and the tonnage of crude steel output?

Geographic Concepts

Geographic Concepts (Glossary of Terms)		
Industrial Revolution	locational interdependence	global division of labor
location theory	primary industrial regions	intermodal connections
variable costs	break-of-bulk point	deindustrialization
friction of distance	Fordist	outsourced
distance decay	post-Fordist	offshore
least cost theory	just-in-time delivery	Sunbelt
agglomeration		Technopole
deglomeration		

Quiz for Geographic Concepts

Match the term with a definition.

1. _____ deglomeration

2. _____ primary industrial regions

3. _____ least cost theory

4. _____ outsource

5. _____ variables costs

A. Places where two or more modes of transportation meet (including air, road, rail, barge and ship).

B. Process by which companies move industrial jobs to other regions with cheaper labor, leaving the region to switch to a service economy and to work through a period of high unemployment.

6. _____ global division of labor

7. _____ just-in-time delivery

8. _____ friction of distance

9. _____ break-of-bulk point

10. _____ technopole

11. _____ intermodal connections

12. _____ offshore

13. _____ Fordist

14. _____ agglomeration

15. _____ deindustrialization

C. A highly organized and specialized system for organizing industrial production and labor; features assembly-line production of standardized components for mass consumption.

D. Process involving the clustering or concentration of people or activities; often refers to manufacturing plants and businesses that benefit from close proximity because they share skilled labor pools and technological and financial amenities.

E. With reference to production, to outsource to a third party located outside of the country.

F. With reference to production, to turn over in part or in total to a third party.

G. Western and Central Europe, Eastern North America, Russia and the Ukraine, East Asia—regions which consist of one or more core areas of industrial development.

H. Method of inventory management made possible by efficient transportation and communication systems, whereby companies keep on hand just what they need for near-term production, planning that what they need for long-term production swill arrive when needed.

I. The increase in time and cost that usually comes with distance.

J. Centers or nodes of high-technology research and activity around which a high-technology corridor is sometimes established.

K. The process of industrial deconcentration in response to technological advances and/or increasing costs due to congestion and competition.

L. A location along a transport route where goods must be transferred from one carrier to another.

M. Phenomenon whereby corporations and others can draw from labor markets around the world, made possible by the compression of time and space through innovation in communication and transportation systems.

N. Costs that change directly with the amount of production (e.g., energy supply and labor costs).

O. Model according to which the location of manufacturing establishments is determined by the minimization of three critical expenses: labor, transportation and agglomeration.

Chapter Related Internet Links

Learn More Online

About the Port of Rotterdam
http://www.portofrotterdam.com

Watch It Online

About Wal-Mart's Influence
http://www.pbs.org/wgbh/pages/frontline/shows/walmart/view/

Exercise for Chapter Related Internet Links

There are several video segments on the PBS site about Wal-Mart. On the above page, choose the segment "Taking the Hits." Discuss the Wal-Mart phenomenon and its business practices, and the impact on TV manufacturers in Ohio and Tennessee.

APHG-Type Questions

Note: Be sure to take the online Self Tests on the Student Companion Site.
Check answer key at the end of the workbook.

Multiple Choice Questions

Type A: Basic Knowledge

1. Over 50% of the goods entering Europe come through two ports in
   A. Luxembourg.
   B. Belgium
   C. Netherlands
   D. Germany
   E. France

2. China's "Pittsburgh" is
   A. Shenyang
   B. Shanghai
   C. Hong Kong
   D. Beijing
   E. Tianjin

3. The second largest industrial district in China developed around _____, China's largest city.
   A. Beijing
   B. Shanghai
   C. Tianjin
   D. Xianggang (Hong Kong)
   E. Dalian

4. Service industries are commonly referred to as _____ industries.
   A. primary
   B. secondary
   C. tertiary
   D. quaternary
   E. quinary

5. Russia's "Detroit" southeast of Moscow:
   A. Kiev
   B. St. Petersburg
   C. Volgograd
   D. Rostov
   E. Nizhni Novgorod

6. Japan's dominant industrial region is
   A. Kitakyushu
   B. Toyama
   C. Kanto Plain
   D. Kansai
   E. Shikoku

7. Fast, flexible production of small lots with outsourcing around the world is referred to as
   A. Fordist
   B. post-Fordist
   C. socialist
   D. colonial production
   E. just-in-time

8. Europe's greatest industrial complex is
   A. Donbas
   B. British Midlands
   C. Silesia
   D. Berlin
   E. the Ruhr

9. The increase in time and cost with distance is referred to as
   A. production costs
   B. distribution costs
   C. friction of distance
   D. distance decay
   E. frustration

10. Burning coal in a near vacuum produced a much hotter burning, pure carbon fuel called
    A. super coal
    B. coke
    C. charcoal
    D. Bessemer fuel
    E. carbonite

Type B: Application

1. England not only held a monopoly over products that were in world demand at the beginning of the Industrial Revolution, but also a monopoly on
   A. international transportation
   B. the sources of raw materials
   C. computer software
   D. all available labor
   E. the skill necessary to make the machines that manufactured the products

2. When Alfred Weber published his book *Theory of the Location of Industries* (1909), what did he select as the critical determinant of regional industrial location?
   A. availability of labor
   B. nearby markets
   C. costs of labor
   D. transportation costs
   E. political influence

3. The type of manufacturing that is more likely to be located in peripheral countries is
   A. technical design
   B. labor-intensive
   C. low-labor needs
   D. high-tech
   E. low value-added

4. The most important locational factor for the service sector is
   A. energy
   B. transportation
   C. market
   D. labor
   E. climate

5. Technopoles, a collection of high-technology industries, can be found in a number of countries. Which of the following is NOT a region containing one of these countries?
   A. Eastern Asia
   B. India
   C. Australia
   D. North America
   E. Africa

Free Response Question

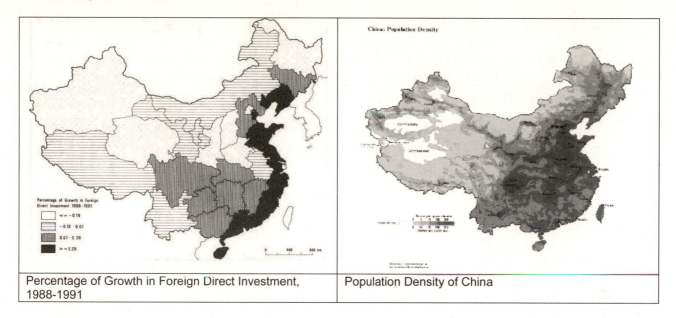

Percentage of Growth in Foreign Direct Investment, 1988-1991	Population Density of China

The map on the left shows the provincial distribution of foreign direct investment (FDI) in China from 1988-1991. The map on the right is a population density map.

Suggest some explanations for the spatial patterns revealed on both maps.

Is there a correlation between population density and foreign investment?

Give at least two possible reasons for the FDI pattern, and two for the population density pattern.

CHAPTER 13: HUMAN ENVIRONMENT

Chapter Summary (from page 439)

What will the future be like? Many would agree with geographer Robert Kates, who foresees a "warmer, more crowded, more connected but diverse world." As we consider this prospect, we must acknowledge that global environmental changes illustrate the limits of our knowledge of the Earth. Many of today's environmental changes were not anticipated. Moreover, many global changes are nonlinear, and some are "chaotic" in the sense that future conditions cannot be reliably predicted. Nonlinearity means that small actions in certain situations may result in large impacts and may be more important than larger actions in causing change. Thresholds also exist in many systems which, once past, are irreversible. This occurs, for example, when the habitat for a species is diminished to the point where the species quickly dies off. Unfortunately, we may not be able to identify these thresholds until we pass them. This leaves open the possibility of "surprises"—unanticipated responses by physical systems.

The complexity and urgency of the environmental challenge will tax the energies of the scientific and policy communities for some time to come. Geography must be an essential part of any serious effort to grapple with these challenges. The major changes that are taking place have different origins and spatial expressions, and each results from a unique combination of physical and social processes. We cannot simply focus on system dynamics and generalized causal relationships. We also consider emerging patterns of environmental change and the impacts of differences from place to place on the operation of general processes. Geography is not the background to the changes taking place; it is at the very heart of the changes themselves.

Key Questions

1. How has the Earth environment changed over time?
2. How have humans impacted the Earth environment?
3. What are the major factors contributing to environmental change today?
4. How are humans responding to environmental change?

Field Notes

(410)   Galle, Sri Lanka. Disaster Along Indian Ocean Shores (tsunami of 2004)

(420)   Tucson, Arizona. Water scarcity in the Southwest.

(424)   Para, Brazil. Destruction of the rainforest.

(428)   Try, Mali. Political ecology as a subfield of geography.

Thinking Geographically

(418) Take time to search the Internet and read about what has happened to Phuket, Thailand, since the Indian Ocean tsunami hit in December 2004. Look for before and after images of Phuket—how did it look before the tsunami hit and after? Research how Phuket has been rebuilt and determine why Phuket has been rebuilt the way it has.

(426) What is the greatest environmental concern facing the region where you live, and in what other regions of the world is this a major concern?

(434) Go back to the last Thinking Geographically question—what is the greatest environmental concern facing the region where you live? Now, add to your answer by concentrating on how people in the community (leaders, students, locals, businesses) discuss this environmental concern. Read newspaper accounts of the debate over this environmental concern. Are the actors in this debate thinking and operating at different scales?

(439) Examine the map of global carbon dioxide emissions and explain the pattern you see. What other geographic patterns are correlated with those shown in the map?

B. Chapter Outline

A.   How Has the Earth Environment Changed Over Time?
   1.   Ocean and Atmosphere
   2.   Fire and Ice
   3.   The Little Ice Age in the Modern Era
B.   How Have Humans Impacted the Earth Environment?
   1.   Alteration of Ecosystems
   2.   Environmental Stress
   3.   Water
      Water Politics in the Middle East
   4.   Atmosphere
      a.   Global Warming
      b.   Acid Rain
   5.   The Land
      a.   Deforestation
      b.   Soil Erosion
      c.   Waste Disposal
   6.   Biodiversity
C.   What Are the Major Factors Contributing to Environmental Change Today?
   1.   Political Ecology
   2.   Population
   3.   Patterns of Consumption
   4.   Technology
   5.   Transportation
      Energy
         Framework Convention on Climate Change
D.   How Are Humans Responding to Environmental Change?
   1.   Biological Diversity
   2.   Protection of the Ozone Layer
   3.   Global Climate Change

Chapter Figures and Tables

Figure	Page	Type	Theme
13.1	389	photo	Galle, Sri Lanka (2004 tsunami damage)
13.2	391	map	World tectonic Plates
13.3	393	illustration	Wegener's Hypothesis of Continental Drift
13.4	394	map	Recent Earthquakes and Volcanic Eruptions
13.5	395	map	Extent of Northern Hemisphere Glaciation During the Late Pleistocene's Wisconsinian Glaciation
13.6	396	photo	Mount Toba, Indonesia (caldera from Toba eruption)
13.7	399	illustration	The Hydrologic Cycle

13.8	400	photo	Tucson, Arizona (bringing water to the desert)
13.9	400	map	The Dying Aral Sea
13.10	401	map	Key Water Resources in the Middle East
13.11	403	photo	Para, Brazil (logging road in the Amazon rain forest)
13.12	404	photo	Guangxi-Zhuang, China (collapse of terracing system)
13.13	407	photo	Try, Mali (cotton harvest in the village of Try)
13.14	408	maps	Natural Disaster Hot Spots
T13.1	409	table	Estimated Liters of Water Required to Produce 1 Kilogram of Food
13.15	410	map	Location of Visible Oil Slicks
13.16	412-413	map	World Distribution of Fossil Fuel Sources
13.17	414	photo	Lake Benton, Minnesota (wind turbines)
13.18	415	map	Major Regions and Forest Zones in Subsaharan Africa
13.19	438	map	Carbon Dioxide Emissions per Capita, 2004
13.20	438	photo	Beijing, China. Urban smog

Exercise for Chapter Figures and Tables

Figure 13.6 is a photograph of the Mount Toba, Indonesia caldera. Read about Mount Toba on the following two wikipedia sites:

- http://en.wikipedia.org/wiki/Toba_eruption
- http://en.wikipedia.org/wiki/Toba_catastrophe_theory

Then read about the Yellowstone supervolcano at:

- http://en.wikipedia.org/wiki/Yellowstone_supervolcano

Discuss the modern day consequences of a Yellowstone eruption if the magnitude of the eruption were similar to past Yellowstone eruptions.

Geographic Concepts

Geographic Concepts (Glossary of Terms)		
chlorofluorocarbons	Holocene	soil erosion
Pangaea	Little Ice Age	solid waste
photosynthesis	environmental stress	sanitary landfills
mass depletions	renewable resources	toxic waste
mass extinctions	hydrologic cycle	radioactive waste
Pacific Ring of Fire	aquifers	biodiversity
Pleistocene	atmosphere	ozone layer
glaciation	global warming	Vienna Convention for the
interglaciation	acid rain	Protection of the Ozone
Wisconsinian glaciation	oxygen cycle	layer
	deforestation	Montreal Protocol

Quiz for Geographic Concepts

Match the term with a definition.

1. _____ aquifers

2. _____ solid waste

3. _____ Montreal Protocol

4. _____ Wisconsinian glaciation

5. _____ mass extinctions

6. _____ toxic waste

7. _____ deforestation

8. _____ Little Ice Age

9. _____ Pleistocene

10. _____ oxygen cycle

11. _____ Pacific Ring of Fire

12. _____ interglaciation

13. _____ radioactive waste

14. _____ ozone layer

15. _____ renewable resources

A. The clearing and destruction of forests to harvest wood for consumption, clear land for agricultural uses, and make way for expanding settlement frontiers.

B. Resources that can regenerate as they are exploited.

C. Hazardous waste causing danger from chemicals and infectious organisms.

D. The layer in the upper atmosphere between 30 and 45 kilometers above the Earth's surface that acts as a filter for the Sun's harmful ultraviolet rays.

E. Mass destruction of most species.

F. Hazardous-waste-emitting radiation from nuclear power plants, nuclear weapons factories, and nuclear equipment in hospitals and industry.

G. The most recent glacial period of the Pleistocene, enduring about 100,000 years and giving way, beginning about 18,000 years ago, to the current interglacial, the Holocene.

H. Sustained warming phase between glaciations during an ice age.

I. An international agreement signed in 1987 that called for a reduction in the production and consumption of chlorofluorocarbons (CFCs) of 50% by 2000.

J. Ocean-girdling zone of crustal instability, volcanism, and earthquakes resulting from the tectonic activity along the plate boundaries in the region.

K. Non-liquid, non-soluble materials raging from municipal garbage to sewage sludge, agricultural refuse, and mining residues.

L. Cycle whereby natural processes and human activity consume atmospheric oxygen and produce carbon dioxide, and the Earth's forests and other flora, through photosynthesis, consume carbon dioxide and produce oxygen.

M. The most recent epoch of the Late Cenozoic Ice Age, beginning 1.8 million years ago, marked by as many as 20 glaciations and interglaciations; the current warm phase has witnessed the rise of human civilization.

N. Subterranean, porous, water-holding rocks that provide millions of wells with steady flows of water.

O. Temporary but significant cooling period between the 14th and 19th centuries, accompanied by wide temperature fluctuations, droughts and storms, causing famines and dislocations.

Chapter Related Internet Links

Learn More Online

About Geography and Environmental Hazards
http://www.bbc.co.uk/scotland/education/int/geog/envhaz/index.shtml

Watch It Online

Surprisingly, the textbook does not have any links for this chapter. Yet there are many audio and visual links that can be streamed from the internet. I suggest you go to these organizations first:

Public Broadcast System (PBS)
http://www.pbs.org/search/

National Public Radio (NPR), All Things Considered
http://www.npr.org/templates/rundowns/rundown.php?prgId=2

On both sites you can search for such key terms as:

global warming   tsunami
earthquake   super volcano

You will find plenty of programs to listen to and/or watch at home or in school.

Exercise for Chapter Related Internet Links

Go to this site:

http://www.pbs.org/wgbh/pages/frontline/shows/reaction/

The program is: "Nuclear Reaction: Why Do Americans Fear Nuclear Power?"

You know the routine. Read, watch, listen, discuss.

Note: Be sure to take the online Self Tests on the Student Companion Site.
Check answer key at the end of the workbook.

Multiple Choice Questions

Type A: Basic Knowledge

1. The Global Environment Facility funds projects related to four issues. Which of the following is not one of these?
    A. loss of biodiversity
    B. climatic change
    C. soil erosion
    D. depletion of the ozone layer
    E. protection of international waters

2. In the early 1980s, the FAO of the United Nations undertook a study of the rate of depletion of tropical rain forests and determined that _____ percent had already been affected by cutting.
    A. 24
    B. 34
    C. 44
    D. 54
    E. 64

3. The United States is the most prolific producer of solid waste. Studies estimate that the U.S. produces about _____ pounds of solid waste per person per day.
    A. 1.5
    B. 3.5
    C. 5.5
    D. 7.3
    E. 8.1

4. The highest densities of coal and oil burning, which causes acid rain, are associated with large concentrations of heavy manufacturing such as those in
    A. southern Africa
    B. coastal South America and Asia
    C. Eastern Europe and East Asia
    D. the Southern Hemisphere
    E. Western and Eastern Europe and the United States

5. The eruption of the Tambora volcano on the island of Sumatra resulted in what has been called the "year without a summer" in Europe and America. That year was
    A. 1000
    B. 1650
    C. 1816
    D. 1912
    E. 1953

6. The world distribution of precipitation is concentrated in
   A. equatorial and tropical areas
   B. mid-latitude regions
   C. high latitudes
   D. subtropical regions
   E. elevations above 5,000 feet

7. The most recent glaciation of the Pleistocene was the _____ Glaciation.
   A. Illinoian
   B. Kansan
   C. Wisconsinian
   D. Nebraskan
   E. New Yorkian

8. The greatest threat to human existence to come from any source was a volcanic eruption occurring about 73,500 years ago. The volcano was called
   A. Santorini
   B. Yellostone
   C. Tambora
   D. Toba
   E. Krakatoa

9. The climatic record documenting the beginning of the Little Ice Age was partially pieced together by using farmer's diaries. Those of _____ were most useful.
   A. dairy farmers
   B. Catholic monks
   C. grain farmers
   D. vegetable growers
   E. wine growers

10. Climatologist-geographer Alfred Wegener used his spatial view of the world to develop the theory of
    A. relativity
    B. the hydrologic cycle
    C. continental-drift
    D. Earth rotation
    E. plate subduction

Type B: Application

1. The boundaries of crustal plates (theory of plate tectonics) are associated with
   A. deserts
   B. earthquakes and volcanoes
   C. ice caps
   D. plains regions
   E. mountain building

2. Plant life and photosynthesis began about 1.5 billion years ago and increased the
   _____ level in the atmosphere.
   A. CO_2
   B. nitrogen
   C. methane
   D. sulfur
   E. O_2

3. Fifty times as much water is stored in _____ in the United States as falls as
   precipitation each year.
   A. reservoirs
   B. aquifers
   C. streams
   D. lakes
   E. glaciers

4. One of the great ecological disasters of the twentieth century occurred in Uzbekistan and
   Kazakhstan and involves the
   A. Black Sea
   B. Lake Baikal
   C. Aral Sea
   D. Caspian Sea
   E. Lake Balqash

5. Forests affect the atmosphere through their role in (the)
   A. global warming
   B. production of CO_2
   C. desertification
   D. oxygen cycle
   E. decomposition

Free Response Question

List three types of alternative energy currently available, and discuss why they or are not being more actively developed.

List two types of alternative energy not yet technologically feasible, but for which science has high hopes for the future.

Give two good reasons why you might oppose building more nuclear (fission) power plants.

CHAPTER 14: GLOBALIZATION AND THE GEOGRAPHY OF NETWORKS

Chapter Summary (from page 454)

Globalization has been compared to a runaway train blowing through stations leaving much of the world to stare at its caboose, but this description is not entirely accurate. Globalization is a series of processes, not all of which are headed in the same direction down a track to a single, united, homogeneous globe. Even the processes headed down the globalization track are often stopped, sent back to the previous station, or derailed. The globalization track is not inevitable or irreversible (in the words of O'Loughlin, Staeheli, and Greenburg). Many of the most important globalization processes take place within networks of global cities (see Chapter 9), of places linked by popular culture (see Chapter 4), of governments (see Chapter 8), of trade (see Chapter 12), and of development (see Chapter 10). At any point along any of these networks are people and places. Just as people make and remake places, people can make and remake globalization.

Key Questions

1. What is globalization, and what role do networks play in globalization?
2. At what scales do networks operate in the globalized world?
3. How have identities changed in a globalized world?

Field Notes

(441)   The Geographies of Global Consumption.

(452)   Columbine, Colorado. Dedication ceremony for the memorial to the victims of the Columbine High School shooting of April 20, 1999 near Littleton, Colorado.

Thinking Geographically

(448) Castells claims that the age of information technology is more revolutionary than either the advent of the printing press or the Industrial Revolution. Determine whether you agree with him, and write an argument in support of your position (use specific examples to support your conclusions).

(451) Think of a place you have been where the global media have worked to create a synergy. Describe the presence of the global media entity in the place and show how the global media have imprinted the cultural landscape of the place and how that imprint affected your experience in (and your sense of) the place?

(454) How does the personalization of tragedy, such as September 11, the Indian Ocean tsunami, or Hurricane Katrina promote both globalization and localization at the same time?

Chapter Outline

A. What is Globalization, and What Role Do Networks Play in Globalization?
    1. Networks
    2. Time-Space Compression
        Global Cities

B. At What Scales Do Networks Operate in the Globalized World?
   1. Networks in Development
      Local Currencies
   2. Networks in Media
      Blogs
   3. Networks of Retail Corporations
C. How Have Identities Changed in a Globalized World?
   Personal Connectedness

Chapter Figures and Tables

Figure	Page	Type	Theme
14.1	441	photo	Gap Clothing.
14.2	443	map	Inside an iPod: The PortalPlayer World.
14.3	444	map	Global Shipping Lanes.
14.4	445	photo	Porto Alegre, Brazil (World Social Forum march)
14.5	446-447	map	World Cities Most Connected to New York City
14.6	449	photo	Bernal Buenos Aires, Argentina
14.7	450	chart	Vertical Integration in the Viacom Corporation
14.8	452	photo	Columbine, Colorado. Memorial to high school shootings.
14.9	453	photo	New York, New York (World Trade Center site in 2002)

Exercise for Chapter Figures and Table

Figure 14.1 and the content of the opening Field Notes reminds me of an exercise I do with my students. I divide the class into small teams, each team being responsible for a category of products, e.g., toys, textiles (and sub-categories of textiles), electronics, tools, etc. Each team is responsible for going to different department stores and determining the country of origin of dozens of products. Sometimes I will have them compare low-cost retail outlets and high-end stores

Geographic Concepts

Geographic Concepts (Glossary of Terms)		
globalization Washington Consensus networks participatory development	local exchange trading system (LETS) vertical integration	synergy gatekeepers horizontal integration

Quiz for Geographic Concepts

Match the term with a definition.

1. _____ vertical integration

2. _____ synergy

3. _____ globalization

4. _____ gatekeepers

A. Ownership by the same firm of a number of companies that exist at the same point on a commodity chain.

B. The expansion of economic, political and cultural processes to the point that they become global in scale and impact; processes that transcend state boundaries and have outcomes that vary across places and scales.

5. _____ participatory development

6. _____ Washington Consensus

7. _____ networks

8. _____ horizontal integration

9. _____ LETS

C. A barter system whereby a local currency is created through which members trade services or goods in a local network separated from the formal economy.

D. Refers to the following fundamentals of free trade: free trade raises the well-being of all countries, and; competition through trade raises a country's long-term growth.

E. Ownership by the same firm of a number of companies that exist along a variety of points on a commodity chain.

F. The cross-promotion of vertically-integrated good.

G. People or corporations who control access to information.

H. The notion that locals should be engaged in deciding what development means for them and how it should be achieved.

I. A set of interconnected nodes without a center.

Chapter Related Internet Links

Learn More Online

About Media Ownership
Columbia Journalism Review's "Who Owns That Website"
http://www.cjr.org/tools/owners

About Media Ownership by the Big Six
http://www.mediachannel.org/ownership/chart.shtml

About the Network of World Cities
http://www.brook.edu/metro/pubs/20050222_worldcities.pdf

About Weblogs
http:www.cir.org/issues/2003/5/blog-welch.asp
http:www.cir.org/issues/2003/5/blogsidebar-welch.asp

About the World Economic Forum
http://www.weform.org/

About the World Social Forum
http://forumsocialmundial.org

Once more the textbook is silent on streaming audio and/or video links. Here's one I like.
Globalization
Marketplace, from American Public Media
http://marketplace.publicradio.org/

Exercise for Chapter Related Internet Links

"Marketplace" is a radio program produced by American Public Media. Go to their homepage, and in the upper right Search box, type "globalization." Several links to previous shows addressing various aspects of globalization appear. Click on those and you get streaming audio. Listen to a few programs, preferably with a world map somewhere nearby. Then, as usual, have a discussion.

APHG-Type Questions

Note: Be sure to take the online Self Tests on the Student Companion Site.
Check answer key at the end of the workbook.

Multiple Choice Questions

Type A: Basic Knowledge

1. According to Manuel Castells, a set of interconnected nodes is a(n)
   A. transport system
   B. circulation manifold
   C. network
   D. communication nexus
   E. synergy

2. The study of global cities showed that _____ is the most globally linked city in the world.
   A. New York
   B. Tokyo
   C. London
   D. Chicago
   E. Miami

3. Corbridge and Kumar's study of participatory development in India found that its greatest success was among
   A. the poorest farmers of a region
   B. landless peasants
   C. better off farmers and particular local groups
   D. urban politicians and business men
   E. NGOs with government subsidies

4. Annual meetings of the World Social Forum—a network of socialist organizations—takes place in
   A. Washington, DC
   B. Buenos Aires, Argentina
   C. Paris, France
   D. Moscow, Russia
   E. Porto Alegre, Brazil

5. The annual meeting of the World Economic Forum—representing large corporations and political leaders of rich countries—takes place in
   A. New York City
   B. Mexico City
   C. Davos, Switzerland
   D. Paris, France
   E. Doha, Qatar

6. More than anything else, globalization is driven by
   A. cultural convergence of media
   B. resource scarcities
   C. population growth
   D. trade
   E. popular culture

7. The idea that locals should be engaged in deciding what development means for them and how to achieve it.
   A. synergy
   B. structuralism
   C. international division of labor
   D. NGO-ization
   E. participatory development

8. When one company, for example an auto parts supplier, buys several similar companies, you have an example of
   A. horizontal integration
   B. vertical integration
   C. a commodity chain
   D. globalization
   E. diseconomies of scale

9. What new technological phenomenon influenced U.S. elections in 2004?
   A. cell phone
   B. instant messaging
   C. CNN online
   D. weblogs
   E. podcasts

10. Refers to the phenomenon in which two or more discrete influences or agents acting together create an effect greater than the sum of the effects each is able to create independently.
    A. synergy
    B. symbiosis
    C. integration
    D. gatekeeping
    E. networking

Type B: Applied

1. Media corporations which integrate ownership in a variety of points along the production and consumption chain are examples of
    A. vertical integration
    B. television networks
    C. longitudinal cooperation
    D. monopolies
    E. diversification

2. Media's power as information gatekeepers has been undercut by
    A. local television stations and newspapers
    B. weblogs on the internet
    C. a decline in newspaper subscription
    D. growth in functional illiteracy
    E. self-censure because of FCC threats about indecency

3. The government of China works with foreign internet companies to limit domestic access to foreign web sites that the government finds threatening—a form of censure is which search engine companies like Google comply. In this role, the government of China is the ultimate
    A. dictator
    B. guardian or morality
    C. agent of change
    D. representative of the will of the people
    E. gatekeeper

4. When you chow down on a bag of Fritos corn chips for breakfast, down a Gatorade sport drink after a soccer game, snack on Cap'n'Crunch after school, and drink Pepsi while doing your homework, besides contributing to bad health, to what else are you contributing with certainty?
    A. outsourcing of manufacturing to China
    B. unemployment in Brazil
    C. the charities these companies support for tax write-offs
    D. the profits of one company, PepsiCo
    E. antiglobalization protests

5. Many antiglobalizationists are opposed to all of the following EXCEPT
    A. increasing government-supported public services
    B. privatization of state-owned entities
    C. the opening of financial markets
    D. liberalization of trade
    E. the encouragement of direct foreign investment

Free Response Question

Capitalism	Globalization	NGO
Developing Countries	G8 or Group of 8	Sweatshop
Fair Trade	IMF	World Bank
Free Trade	NAFTA	World Trade Organization

Choose any four of the above globalization-related terms. For each, write a brief description of the perspective taken by both globalization supporters and antiglobalizationists.

Photos from Charles Fuller's Personal Collection

Patan, Nepal

Multilingual street urchins.

These art students were conversant in English, German, French and Chinese Mandarin. I did not have any other languages with which to test them.

New Delhi, India

Don't leave home without them.

These credit card logos on a store in New Delhi speak volumes about globalization and global intercon-nectedness.

Mathura, India

Rural roadside rest stop.

Pepsi
(United States)

Samsung
(South Korea)

Bisleri
(India)

Jaipur, India

McWaste.

In a land where beef consumption is anathema for most of the people, here lies a symbol of fast food beef consumption. A symbol, also, of tropical rainforest deforestation in Brazil.

Appendix 1

Thinking Geographically (Summary)

Thinking Geographically		
Chapter	**Section Title**	**Comment-Question**
1	What is Human Geography?	Imagine and Describe the most remote place on Earth you can think of 100 years ago. Now describe how globalization has changed this place and how the people there continue to shape it—to make it the place it is today.
	What Are Geographic Questions?	Geographers who practice fieldwork keep their eyes open to the world around them and through practice become adept at reading cultural landscapes. Take a walk around your campus or town and try reading the cultural landscape. Choose one thing in the cultural landscape and ask yourself, "what is that and why is it there?" Take the time to find out the answer.
	Why Do Geographers Use Maps, And What Do Maps Tell Us?	Give a friend or family member a blank piece of paper. Ask the person to draw a detailed map of how he or she gets from home to the place where most of his or her weekdays are spent (work, school). Note the age of the person and the length of time he or she has lived in the place and traveled the route. Analyze the map for terra incognita, landmarks, paths, and accessibility. What does the map reveal about the person's lifestyle and activity space?
	Why Are Geographers Concerned With Scale And Connectedness?	Once you think about different types of diffusion, you will be tempted to figure out what kind of diffusion is taking place for all sorts of goods, ideas, or diseases. Please remember any good, idea, or disease can diffuse in more than one way. Choose a good, idea, or disease as an example and describe how it diffused from its hearth across the globe, referring to at least three different types of diffusion.
	What Are Geographic Concepts, And How Are They Used In Answering Geographic Questions?	Create a strong (false) statement about a people and their environment using either environmental determinism or possibilism. Determine how the statement you wrote is false, taking into consideration the roles of culture, politics, and economy in human – environment relations.
2	Where In The World Do People Live And Why?	As we discussed in the field note at the beginning of this chapter, populations are falling in some parts of the world. How will Figure 2.5 look different 50 years from now? If you were updating this textbook in 50 years, where would the largest population clusters in the world be?
	Why Do Populations Rise or Fall In Particular Places?	Examine Appendix B at the end of the book. Study the growth rate column. Which countries have the highest growth rates? Determine what stage of the demographic transition these countries are in, and hypothesize what may lead them to the next stage.

	Why Does Population Composition Matter?	In the United States, the national infant mortality rate (IMR) is 7.0. That number represents and average for the country. Think about the differences in IMR in the United States across regions, ethnicities, social classes, and other sectors. Hypothesize what the differences are—where and for whom is IMR highest and lowest and why? Use the population Internet sites listed at the end of this chapter to determine whether your hypotheses are correct.
	How Do Governments Affect Population Change?	When studying government policies on population, one of the most important things to remember is unintended consequences. Choose one country in the world where women have little access to education and are disempowered. Consider the previous section of this chapter on age composition, and determine how restrictive population policies in this country will alter the population composition of the country.
3	What Is Migration?	Choose one type of cyclic or periodic movement and then think of a specific example of the kind of movement you chose. Now, determine how this movement changes both the home and the destination. How do these places change as a result of this cyclic or period movement?
	Why Do People Migrate?	Think about migration flow within your family, whether internal, international, voluntary, or forced. The flow can be one you experience or one you only heard about through family. List the push and pull factors. Then, write a letter in the first person (if you were not involved, pretend you were your grandmother or whomever) to another family member at "home" describing how you came to migrate to the destination.
	Where Do People Migrate?	Imagine you are from an extremely poor country, and you earn less than $1 a day. Choose a country to be from, and look for it on a map. Assume you are a voluntarily migrant. You look at your access to transportation and the opportunities you have to go elsewhere. Be realistic, and describe how you determine where you will go, how you get there, and what you do once you get there.
	How Do Governments Affect Migration?	One goal of international organizations involved in aiding refugees is repatriation—return of the refugees to their home countries once the threat against them has passed. Take the example of Sudanese refugees. Think about how their land and their lives have changed since they became refugees. You are assigned the daunting task of repatriating Sudanese from Uganda once a peace solution is reached. What steps would you have to take to re-discover a home for these refugees?
4	What Are Local And Popular Cultures?	Employing the concept of hierarchical diffusion, describe how you became a "knower" of your favorite kind of music— where is its hearth, and how did it reach you?

		How Are Local Cultures Sustained?	What is the last place you went to or the last product you purchased that claimed to be "authentic?" What are the challenges of defending the authenticity of this place or product while refuting the authenticity of other similar places or products?
		How Is Popular Culture Diffused?	Thinking about your local community (your college campus, your neighborhood, or your town). Determine how your local community takes one aspect of popular culture and makes it your own.
		How Can Local and Popular Cultures Be Seen In The Cultural Landscape?	Focus on the cultural landscape of your college campus. Think about the concept of placelessness. Determine whether your campus is a "placeless place" or if the cultural landscape of your college reflects the unique identity of the place. Imagine you are hired to build a new student union on your campus. How could you design the building to reflect the uniqueness of your college?
5		What Is Identity, And How Are Identities Constructed?	Recall the last time you were asked to check a box for your "race." Does that box factor into how you make sense of yourself locally, regionally, nationally, and globally?
		How Do Places Affect Identity, And How Can We See Identities In Places?	In the 2000 census, the government tallied the number of *households* where a same-sex couple (with or without children) lived. Study the map of same-sex households by census tract in Figure 5.10. What gay men and lesbian women are not being counted on this map? How would the map change if sexuality were one of the "boxes" *every* person filled out on the census?
		How Do Power Relationships Subjugate Certain Groups Of People?	Geographers who study race, ethnicity, gender, or sexuality are interested in the power relationships embedded in a place from which assumptions about "others" are formed or reinforced. Consider your own place, your campus, or locality. What power relationships are embedded in this place?
6		What Are Languages, And What Role Do Languages Play In Cultures?	Linguist Bert Vaux's study of dialects in American English points to the differences in words for common things such as soft drinks and sandwiches. Describe a time when you said something and a speaker of another dialect did not understand the word you used. Was the word a term for a common thing? Why do you think dialects have different words for common things, things found across dialects, such as soft drinks and sandwiches?
		Why Are Languages Distributed The Way They Are?	Education also affects the distribution of languages across the globe and within regions and countries. Thinking about different regions of the world, consider how education plays a role in the distribution of English speakers. Who learns English in each of these regions and why? What role does education play in the global distribution of English speakers?
		How Do Languages Diffuse?	Choose a country in the world. Imagine you become a strong leader of a centralized government in the country. Pick a language other than a current language spoken in the

		country. Determine what policies you could put in place to replace the country's language with the new language. How many years, or how many generations, would need to pass before your program achieves your desired outcome?
	What Role Does Language Play In Making Places?	*This place was first named by Gabrielino Indians. In 1769, Spanish Franciscan priests renamed the place. In 1850, English speakers renamed the place.* Do not use the Internet to help you. Use only maps in this book or in atlases to help you deduce what this place is. Maps of European exploration and colonialism will help you the most. Look at the end of the chapter summary for the answer.
7	What Is Religion, And What Role Does It Play In Culture?	Describe how religion and language affect and change each other to shape cultures. (Consider what happens to a society's religion and language when a different religion or language diffuses to the place.)
	Where Did The Major Religions Of The World Originate, And How Do Religions Diffuse?	Migration plays a large role in the diffusion of religions, both universalizing and ethnic. As Europe becomes more secular, migrants from outside of Europe continue to settle in the region. Imagine Europe 30 years from now. Predict where in Europe secularism will be the most prominent and where religious adherence will strengthen.
	How Is Religion Seen In The Cultural Landscape?	Choose a pilgrimage site, such as Mecca, Vatican City, or the Western Wall, and describe how the act of pilgrimage (in some cases by millions) alters this place's cultural landscape and environment.
	What Role Does Religion Play In Political Conflicts?	Boal's studies in Northern Ireland demonstrate that solving a religious conflict is typically not about theology; it is about identity. You are assigned the potentially Nobel Prize–winning task of "solving" the conflict either in Northern Ireland or in Israel and Palestine. Using Boal's example, determine how you can alter activity spaces and change identities to create the conditions for long-lasting peace in one of these major conflict zones.
8	How Is Space Politically Organized Into States and Nations?	Imagine you are the leader of a newly independent state in Africa or Asia. Determine what your government can do to build a nation that corresponds with the borders of your state. Consider the roles of education, government, military, and culture in your exercise in nation-building.
	How Do States Spatially Organize Their Governments?	Choose an example of a devolutionary movement and determine whether autonomy (self-governance) for that region would benefit the autonomous region, the country in which it is located, or both.
	How Are Boundaries Established, And Why Do Boundary Disputes Occur?	People used to think physical-political boundaries were more stable than geometric boundaries. Through many studies of many places, political geographers have confirmed that this idea is false. Construct your own argument explaining why physical-political boundaries can create just as much instability as geometric boundaries.

		How Do Geopolitics and Critical Geopolitics Help Us Understand The World?	Read a major newspaper (in print or online) and look for a recent statement by a world political leader regarding international politics. Using the concept of critical geopolitics, determine what view of the world the world leader has—how he/she defines the world spatially.
		What Are Supranational Organizations, And What Is The Future Of The State?	In 2004, the European Union welcomed 10 additional states, and in 2007, the European Union plans to welcome 2 more states. Examine the European Union website (listed below in the Learn More Online section). Read about the European Union's expansion and what is going on in the European Union right now. Consider how complicated it is for the European Union to bring together these many divergent members into one supranational organization.
9		When And Why Did People Start Living In Cities?	Archaeologists have found that the houses in Indus River cities, such as Mohenjo-Daro and Harappa, were a uniform size: each house had access to a sewer system, and palaces were absent from the cultural landscape. Derive a theory as to why these conditions were present in these cities that had both a leadership class and a surplus of agricultural goods.
		Where Are Cities Located And Why?	Sketch a map of your city or town and the cities or towns nearby. Make a list of the kinds of goods and services available in each of these towns. Do the ideas about central places presented in this section of the chapter apply to your region?
		How Are Cities Organized, And How Do They Function?	Employing the concepts defined in this section of the chapter, draw a model of the city with which you are most familiar. Label each section of the city accordingly. After reading through the models described in this section, determine which model best corresponds to the model you drew and hypothesize as to why it is so.
		How Do People Make Cities?	Using the city you sketched in the last "Thinking Geographically" question, consider the concepts and processes introduced in this section of the chapter and explain how people and institutions created this city and the model you sketched.
		What Role Do Cities Play In Globalization?	Thinking through the challenges to the state presented in Chapter 8, predict whether and under what circumstances world cities could replace states as the basic and most powerful form of political organization in the world.
10		How Do You Define And Measure Development?	Is the idea of economic development inherently Western? If the West (North America and Europe) were not encouraging the "developing world" to "develop," how would people in the regions of the "developing world" think about their own economies?
		How Does Geography Affect Development?	Compare and contrast Rostow's ladder of development with Wallerstein's three-tier structure of the world economy.

	What Are The Barriers To And The Costs Of Economic Development?	Think of a trip you have made to a poorer area of the country or a poorer region of the world. Describe how your experience in the place as a tourist was fundamentally different from the everyday lives of the people who live in the place.
	Why Do Countries Experience Uneven Development Within The State?	Take an item of clothing out of your closet, and using the Internet, try to trace the commodity chain of production. What steps did the item go through before reaching you? Consider whether core or peripheral processes were operating at each step and consider the roles governments and international political regimes played along each step.
11	What Is Agriculture, And Where Did Agriculture Begin?	Settling down in one place, a rising population, and the switch to agriculture are interrelated occurrences in human history. Hypothesize which of these three happened first, second, and third and explain why.
	How Did Agriculture Change With Industrialization?	Genetically engineered crops are yielding some ethical problems. In the semi-periphery and periphery, farmers typically keep seeds from crops so that they can plant the seeds the next year. Companies that produce genetically engineered seeds do not approve of this process; generally, they want farmers to purchase new seeds each year. Using the concepts of scale and jumping scale, determine the ethical questions in this debate.
	What Imprint Does Agriculture Make On The Cultural Landscape?	Think of an agricultural region you have either visited or seen from an airplane. Describe the imprint of agriculture on this cultural landscape and consider what the cultural landscape tells you about how agriculture is produced in this region and how production has changed over time.
12	Where Did The Industrial Revolution Begin, And How Did It Diffuse?	Examine the map of diffusion of the Industrial Revolution into Europe and determine what other characteristics (aside from presence of coal) were necessary for industrialization to take hold in these regions.
	How Do Location Theories Explain Industrial Location?	Think of an industrial area where you live, either an industrial park or a major conglomeration of industries. Drive through the area or look online or in the phone book to see what industries are located there. Consider the models of industrial location described in this section of the chapter and determine whether any of the models apply to this place.
	How Has Industrial Production Changed?	Think about a cutting-edge, high-technology product that is still quite expensive to purchase and not yet broadly used (perhaps something you have read about but not even seen). Using the Internet, determine where this product is manufactured and assess why the product is manufactured there. Hypothesize which countries production will shift to and how long it will take for production costs (and the price of the product) to decrease substantially.

	Where Are The Major Industrial Belts In The World Today And Why?	How does a place change when deindustrialization occurs? Consider a place that has experienced deindustrialization, and research recent news articles on the Internet to find out how the economy of the place has changed since the loss of industry. What has happened to the place and its economy?
	What Is The Service Economy, And Where Are Services Concentrated?	What majors are most popular at your college or university? Consider what service/high-technology corridors may already exist near your college or university. Propose (where, why, how) a new service/high-technology corridor for your region based on what your college/university has to offer the industry.
13	How Has The Earth Environment Changed Over Time?	Take time to search the internet and read about what has happened to Phuket, Thailand, since the Indian Ocean tsunami hit in December 2004. Imagine how the cultural landscape of Phuket has changed and describe whether you think "layers" of the place and its history can still be seen in the cultural landscape (look for images to inspire your thoughts).
	How Have Humans Impacted The Earth Environment?	What is the greatest environmental concern facing the region where you live, and in what other regions of the world is this a major concern?
	What Are The Major Factors Contributing To Environmental Change Today?	Go back to the last Thinking Geographically question—what is the greatest environmental concern facing the region where you live? Now, add to your answer by concentrating on how people in the community (leaders, students, locals, businesses) discuss this environmental concern. Read newspaper accounts of the debate over this environmental concern. Are the actors in this debate thinking and/or operating at different scales?
	How Are Humans Responding To Environmental Change?	Examine the map of global carbon dioxide emissions and explain the pattern you see on the map.
14	What Is Globalization, And What Role Do Networks Play In Globalization?	Castells claims that the age of information technology is more revolutionary than either the advent of the printing press or the Industrial Revolution. Determine whether you agree with him, and write an argument in support of your position (use specific examples to support your conclusions).
	At What Scales Do Networks Operate In The Globalized World?	Think of a place you have been where the global media have worked to create a synergy. Describe the presence of the global media entity in the place and show how the global media have imprinted the cultural landscape of the place and how that imprint affected your experience in (and your sense of) the place?
	How Have Identities Changed In A Globalized World?	How does the personalization of tragedy, such as September 11, the Indian Ocean tsunami, or Hurricane Katrina promote both globalization and localization at the same time?

Appendix 2: Bibliography/Works Cited

Annan, Kofi. 2001. Secretary-General Asks United States Geographers To Work With Him To Tackle Climate Change Problems, Environmental Degradation And Sustainable Development. http://www.unis.unvienna.org/unis/pressrels/2001/sgsm7732.html.

Bailey, Adrian. 2006. What Kind of Assessment for What Kind of Geography? Advanced Placement Human Geography. *The Professional Geographer*. 58:70-77.

College Board. 2002. *Advanced Placement Human Geography: 2001 Released Exam*. New York: College Board.

College Board. 2006. *Advance Placement Human Geography Course Description*. New York: College Board.

de Blij, H. J., et al. 2007. *Human Geography: People, Place, and Culture*. Hoboken: John Wiley & Sons.

Dewey, Russell A. Writing Multiple Choice Items which Require Comprehension. http://www.psywww.com/selfquiz/aboutq.htm

Geography Education Standards Project. 1994. *Geography for Life: National Geography Standards*. Washington, D.C.: National Geographic Research & Exploration.

Peterson, Michael P. The Importance of Geography. http://maps.unomaha.edu/Peterson/presentations/Charting/Importance.html

Rubenstein, James M. 2008. *An Introduction to Human Geography: The Cultural Landscape*. Upper Saddle River: Pearson/Prentice Hall.

ANSWER KEY

CHAPTER 1: Introduction To Human Geography

Quiz for Geographic Concepts		**APHG-Type M/C Questions** Basic Knowledge		**APHG-Type M/C Questions** Application	
1.	E	1.	D	1.	B
2.	F	2.	E	2.	E
3.	B	3.	E	3.	A
4.	K	4.	C	4.	A
5.	H	5.	E	5.	B
6.	N	6.	D		
7.	G	7.	E		
8.	L	8.	A		
9.	M	9.	C		
10.	A	10.	B		
11.	J				
12.	D				
13.	C				
14.	O				
15.	I				

CHAPTER 2: Population

Quiz for Geographic Concepts		**APHG-Type M/C Questions** Basic Knowledge		**APHG-Type M/C Questions** Application	
1.	I	1.	D	1.	B
2.	J	2.	E	2.	A
3.	D	3.	A	3.	E
4.	N	4.	E	4.	A
5.	E	5.	D	5.	E
6.	G	6.	A		
7.	H	7.	B		
8.	B	8.	B		
9.	O	9.	E		
10.	C	10.	C		
11.	M				
12.	F				
13.	L				
14.	K				
15.	A				

CHAPTER 3: Migration

Quiz for Geographic Concepts

1. I
2. K
3. B
4. A
5. N
6. J
7. M
8. D
9. E
10. O
11. L
12. C
13. H
14. G
15. F

APHG-Type M/C Questions
Basic Knowledge

1. D
2. C
3. A
4. E
5. A
6. B
7. E
8. C
9. A
10. A

APHG-Type M/C Questions
Application

1. D
2. A
3. E
4. C
5. E

CHAPTER 4: Local Culture, Popular Culture, And Cultural Landscapes

Quiz for Geographic Concepts

1. C
2. O
3. H
4. E
5. L
6. D
7. K
8. N
9. J
10. F
11. G
12. I
13. B
14. M
15. A

APHG-Type M/C Questions
Basic Knowledge

1. D
2. A
3. E
4. C
5. A
6. D
7. C
8. D
9. C
10. E

APHG-Type M/C Questions
Application

1. E
2. B
3. D
4. E
5. E

CHAPTER 5: Identity: Race, Ethnicity, Gender, And Sexuality

Quiz for Geographic Concepts

1. B
2. I
3. N
4. A
5. C
6. J
7. H
8. O
9. G
10. K
11. F
12. L
13. E
14. M
15. D

APHG-Type M/C Questions
Basic Knowledge

1. E
2. A
3. B
4. D
5. A
6. B
7. E
8. C
9. D
10. E

APHG-Type M/C Questions
Application

1. B
2. E
3. D
4. B
5. E

CHAPTER 6: Language

Quiz for Geographic Concepts

1. J
2. N
3. M
4. F
5. G
6. H
7. O
8. L
9. D
10. E
11. I
12. K
13. C
14. B
15. A

APHG-Type M/C Questions
Basic Knowledge

1. D
2. A
3. E
4. C
5. B
6. E
7. B
8. D
9. C
10. C

APHG-Type M/C Questions
Application

1. E
2. A
3. C
4. B
5. B

CHAPTER 7: Religion

Quiz for Geographic Concepts

1. A
2. K
3. B
4. L
5. C
6. M
7. H
8. G
9. N
10. J
11. F
12. I
13. E
14. O
15. D

APHG-Type M/C Questions Basic Knowledge

1. B
2. B
3. C
4. C
5. E
6. D
7. D
8. A
9. A
10. E

APHG-Type M/C Questions Application

1. A
2. B
3. A
4. D
5. E

CHAPTER 8: Political Geography

Quiz for Geographic Concepts

1. H
2. K
3. I
4. B
5. A
6. J
7. N
8. D
9. M
10. L
11. C
12. F
13. O
14. G
15. E

APHG-Type M/C Questions Basic Knowledge

1. C
2. A
3. E
4. D
5. D
6. D
7. A
8. B
9. E
10. D

APHG-Type M/C Questions Application

1. C
2. C
3. C
4. C
5. E

CHAPTER 9: Urban Geography

Quiz for Geographic Concepts

1. C
2. L
3. F
4. A
5. K
6. O
7. N
8. B
9. G
10. H
11. J
12. E
13. M
14. I
15. D

APHG-Type M/C Questions
Basic Knowledge

1. C
2. A
3. B
4. E
5. B
6. B
7. C
8. B
9. A
10. A

APHG-Type M/C Questions
Application

1. E
2. C
3. A
4. A
5. A

CHAPTER 10: Development

Quiz for Geographic Concepts

1. B
2. A
3. M
4. G
5. I
6. N
7. D
8. C
9. J
10. H
11. O
12. F
13. E
14. L
15. K

APHG-Type M/C Questions
Basic Knowledge

1. C
2. A
3. E
4. A
5. A
6. D
7. B
8. D
9. E
10. A

APHG-Type M/C Questions
Application

1. B
2. D
3. C
4. A
5. E

CHAPTER 11: Agriculture

Quiz for Geographic Concepts

1. B
2. H
3. F
4. O
5. G
6. L
7. M
8. C
9. K
10. D
11. N
12. E
13. J
14. I
15. A

APHG-Type M/C Questions
Basic Knowledge

1. D
2. E
3. B
4. B
5. D
6. C
7. E
8. B
9. C
10. B

APHG-Type M/C Questions
Application

1. A
2. B
3. C
4. C
5. E

CHAPTER 12: Industry And Service

Quiz for Geographic Concepts

1. K
2. G
3. O
4. F
5. N
6. M
7. H
8. I
9. L
10. J
11. A
12. E
13. C
14. D
15. B

APHG-Type M/C Questions
Basic Knowledge

1. C
2. A
3. B
4. C
5. E
6. C
7. B
8. E
9. C
10. B

APHG-Type M/C Questions
Application

1. E
2. D
3. B
4. C
5. E

CHAPTER 13: HUMAN ENVIRONMENT

Quiz for Geographic Concepts

1. N
2. K
3. I
4. G
5. E
6. C
7. A
8. O
9. M
10. L
11. J
12. H
13. F
14. D
15. B

APHG-Type M/C Questions
Basic Knowledge

1. C
2. C
3. B
4. E
5. C
6. A
7. C
8. D
9. E
10. C

APHG-Type M/C Questions
Application

1. B
2. E
3. B
4. C
5. D

CHAPTER 14: GLOBALIZATION AND THE GEOGRAPHY OF NETWORKS

Quiz for Geographic Concepts

1. E
2. F
3. B
4. G
5. H
6. D
7. I
8. A
9. C

APHG-Type M/C Questions
Basic Knowledge

1. C
2. C
3. C
4. E
5. C
6. D
7. E
8. A
9. D
10. A

APHG-Type M/C Questions
Application

1. A
2. B
3. E
4. D
5. A